EXECUTIVE EDITORS
Mike Mifsud, Alan Doan, Jenny Doan,
Sarah Galbraith, David Mifsud

MANAGING EDITOR
Natalie Earnheart

CREATIVE DIRECTOR
Christine Ricks

PHOTOGRAPHY TEAM
Mike Brunner, Lauren Dorton, Jennifer Dowling,
Dustin Weant

PATTERN TEAM
Edie McGinnis, Denise Lane, Jessica Toye,
Tyler MacBeth

PROJECT DESIGN TEAM
Jenny Doan, Natalie Earnheart, Janet Yamamoto

EDITOR & COPYWRITERS
Jenny Doan, Natalie Earnheart, Katie Mifsud,
Camille Maddox, Nichole Spravzoff, Julie Barber,
David Litherland, Edie McGinnis

SEWIST TEAM
Jenny Doan, Natalie Earnheart, Janet Yamamoto,
Carol Henderson, Denise Lane, Janice Richardson,
Jamey Stone

QUILTING & BINDING DEPARTMENT
Ren Eide, Becky Bowen, Sandy Childs, Amy Turpin,
Nikki LaPiana, Debbie Allen, Victoria Swieger, Glenda
Rorabough, Bernice Kelly, Deloris Burnett, Darlene
Smith, Todd Harman, Debbie Elder, Jessica Paup, Jan
Meek, Kristin Cash, Lois Eckerts, Natalie Loucks, Holly
Clevenger, Willie Morgan, Linda Frump, Nora Clutter,
Lyndia Lovell, Rachael Joyce, Leta Eaton, Roxana
Hinkle, Jackie Jones, Salena Smiley, Francesca Fleming

LOCATION CREDIT
Billie Mcgraw, Hamilton Elementary School
Scott & Fran Esrey Hamilton Mo.
Rick A.D & Cindy Ross Kidder Mo.
Ken & Janet Richardson Kidder Mo.

PRINTING COORDINATORS
Rob Stoebener, Seann Dwyer

PRINTING SERVICES
Walsworth Print Group
803 South Missouri
Marceline, MO 64658

CONTACT US
Missouri Star Quilt Company
114 N Davis
Hamilton, MO 64644
888-571-1122
info@missouriquiltco.com

content

Oops! Sometimes we make mistakes.
To find corrections to every issue of Block
go to: **www.msqc.co/corrections**

hello
from MSQC

When the first crisp breezes start to blow through town, I feel invigorated after a drowsy summer spent in the sunshine. The overcast skies make all the colorful leaves seem brighter, and I practically rejoice when the rains come again to refresh the dry land. Fall comes and goes quickly, but for the glorious moment that it's here, I can't help but think it's the most exciting time to be alive.

Fall marks the beginning of what I like to call "quilting season." As soon as the first frost comes along, quilting becomes an absolute pleasure with the promise of a cozy winter. It's also the perfect time to plan your next charity project, remembering those who would benefit so much from your kindness.

Fall is ultimately a time for gratitude and for sharing the plenty that we have. The beauty all around us is emphasized by the deeper things that make our lives meaningful. Love can be expressed in many forms, and one of my favorite ways to show I care is by wrapping up someone I adore with a handmade quilt. Thank you for spreading the love and making the world a more beautiful place.

Jenny

JENNY DOAN
MISSOURI STAR QUILT CO

TRY OUR APP

It's easy to keep up on every issue of BLOCK magazine. Access it from all your devices. And when you subscribe to BLOCK, it's free with your subscription! For the app, search BLOCK magazine in the app store. Available for both Apple and Android.

For the tutorial and everything you need to make this quilt visit:
www.msqc.co/blockfall18

54-40 or fight freestyle

A visit to Hamilton, Missouri, isn't complete without a quick stop at the nearby Amish community, Jamesport. Just thirty minutes north from the shops at Missouri Star, this quaint little town is a treasure from another era just waiting to be explored.

Visitors enjoy shopping for hand-crafted baskets and furniture, sampling delicious home-baked goods, and hunting for treasure in the local antique shops. They may also take a peek in the two quilt shops to see what they have to offer. The Amish ladies in this community are accomplished quilters, and they do all their work by hand or with a foot-powered treadle sewing machine.

Jamesport is the largest Old Order Amish community west of the Mississippi River, and it's one of the strictest. The people abide by a rigid code of simple living and plain dress. Women wear long, modest dresses in muted colors. They let their hair grow long, but it is always pulled up and covered with a tight-fitted white bonnet called a kapp. Men wear button-up trousers with suspenders, solid shirts, untrimmed beards, and wide-brimmed straw hats.

Technology such as telephones, automobiles, and electricity are rejected in favor of simplicity and hard work. Families travel by horse and buggy, and fields are plowed without self-propelled machinery. Every aspect of the culture is intended to avoid pride and promote unity. They are a close-knit community, and they depend on one another for support.

When a member of the community is faced with a particularly daunting task, he invites his friends over for a traditional Amish "frolic." The entire neighborhood comes to the rescue, so whether they're building a fence or raising a barn, they are able to complete the work in a fraction of the time.

Often during a frolic, the men do the hard labor while the women prepare a hearty feast and older children look after the

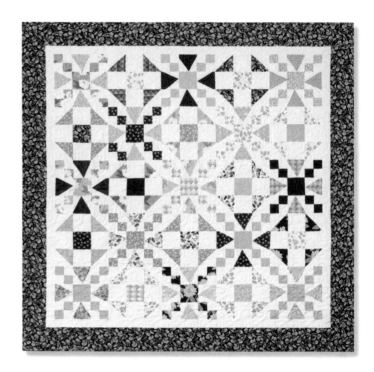

little ones. Everyone pitches in, and as one man's burden is lifted, it is transformed into a delightful social event for the entire community. After all, many hands make light work—and light work isn't half bad!

These frolics provide wonderful opportunities for the community to build strong bonds of fellowship and unity. As they work together, their hearts are stitched together like the pieces of a beautiful quilt.

Over the years, I have come to admire so many things about my Amish neighbors. I marvel at their ability to hold tight to simplicity in the face of an ever more complicated world. But above all, it is the dedication to friends, family, and the common good that make Jamesport such a special place.

materials

QUILT SIZE
75" x 75"

BLOCK SIZE
12" finished

QUILT TOP
1 package of 10" print squares
3¼ yards background fabric
  - includes inner border

OUTER BORDER
1½ yards

BINDING
¾ yard

BACKING
4¾ yards - vertical seam(s)

SAMPLE QUILT
Twilight by One Canoe Two for
Moda Fabrics

1 cut

From the background fabric, cut:

- (13) 5" strips across the width of the fabric
  - subcut each strip into 5" squares. Each
  strip will yield 8 squares and a **total of 102**
  are needed.

- (6) 4½" strips across the width of the fabric
  – subcut each strip into 4½" squares. Each
  strip will yield 8 squares and a **total of 48**
  are needed.

Set aside the remaining fabric for the inner
border.

Note: As you cut the following pieces from the
print 10" squares, stack all matching pieces
together.

From each of 13 print 10" squares, cut:

- (4) 5" squares – trim 2 of the squares
  to 4½"

From each of 13 print 10" squares, cut:

- (4) 4½" squares

From each of 6 print 10" squares, cut:

- (4) 5" squares

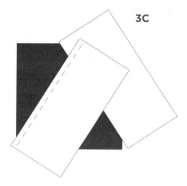

2A

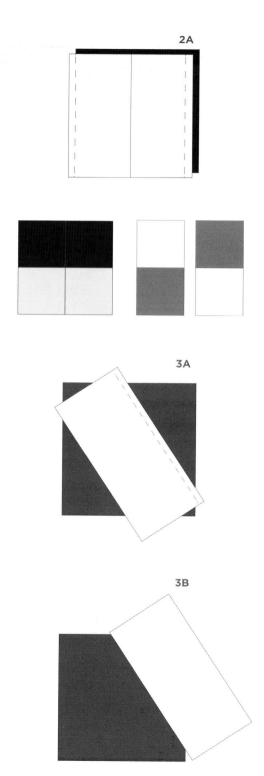

3A

3B

3C

3D

remaining matching print square and the background square. You should have 4 matching 4-patch blocks. **Make 13** matching sets of 4-patches. **2A**

3 outer center units

Pick up 4 matching 4½" squares and 4 background 5" squares. Cut the background squares in half to make (8) 2½" x 5" rectangles. Fold a 4½" print square in half and finger press a crease in place to mark the halfway point. Place a 2½" x 5" background rectangle over the crease with right sides facing so it overlaps the center by about ¼". Sew a rectangle to the square at an angle (any angle will do!) with right sides facing, using a ¼" seam allowance. Press the strip toward the outside edge of the square. **3A 3B**

Repeat, sewing a strip to the other side of the print square. Press the strip toward the outer edge of the square. Square the block to 4½". **3C 3D**

Note: As you stitch each strip to the square, you can trim the excess fabric away ¼" from each seam allowance as you go, or you can simply leave it in place. It doesn't add much bulk. **Make 13** matching sets of these units.

2 make 4-patches

Pick up 2 matching 5" squares and 2 background 5" squares. Layer a 5" background square with a 5" print square. Sew on 2 sides of the layered squares. Measure in 2½" from the outside edge of the seam allowance and cut through the sewn squares vertically. Open each side and press the seam allowance toward the darker fabric. Again, cut through the center, measuring 2½" in from the outer edge. Turn 1 piece so a print aligns with a background piece and sew the 2 together to create a 4-patch as shown. Repeat using the

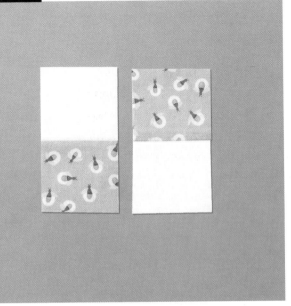

1 Sew (2) 2-patches together to make a 4-patch unit. Make 4 per block.

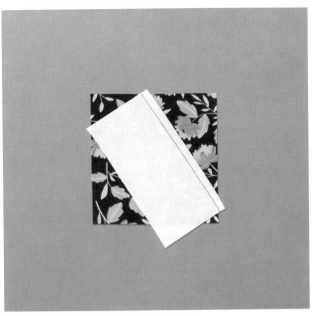

2 Fold a 4½" square in half and finger press a crease in place to mark the halfway point. Place a 2½" x 5" background rectangle over the crease with right sides facing so it overlaps the center by at least ¼". Sew the rectangle to the square at an angle (any angle will work) using a ¼" seam allowance.

3 Add another 2½" x 5" rectangle to the other side of the square with right sides facing.

4 Square the unit to 4½". Make 4 per block.

5 Sew a 4-patch unit to either side of a center unit to make the top and bottom row. Sew a center unit to either side of a 4½" square that matches the print used for the 4-patches to make the center row. Sew all 3 rows together to complete the block.

6 Make Shoo Fly blocks by sewing a half-square triangle unit to either side of a background 4½" square to make the top and bottom row. Sew a 4½" background square to either side of a 4½" print square to make the center row. Sew the rows together to complete the block.

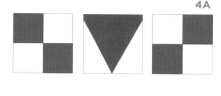

4A

4B

4C

5A

6A

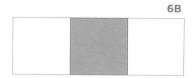

6B

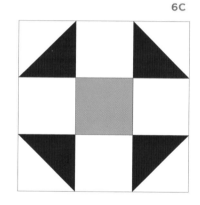

6C

4 block construction

Pick up 4 matching 4-patch units and a matching 4½" square. You'll also need 4 other matching center units. Notice that the outer units don't match the 4-patches or the center square.

Sew a 4-patch to either side of a center unit. **Make 2 rows** like this. **4A**

Sew a center unit to either side of a 4½" square that matches the print used for the 4-patches. **Make 1 row** like this. **4B**

Sew the 3 rows together to complete (1) 54-40 or Fight block. **Make 13. 4C**

5 make half-square triangles

Pick up 2 matching 5" squares and 2 background 5" squares. Draw a line from corner to corner once on the diagonal on the reverse side of the background squares. Layer a background square with a print square. Sew on both sides of the line using a ¼" seam allowance. Cut on the drawn line, then open to reveal 2 half-square triangle units. Repeat to make 2 more half-square triangles. You'll need 4 matching half-square triangles for each block for a total 12 sets. Square each to 4½". **5A**

6 block construction

Pick up a set of 4 matching half-square triangles, 4 background 4½" squares and 1 print 4½" square. Sew a half-square triangle unit to either side of a background 4½" square. **Make 2 rows** like this. **6A**

Sew a 4½" background square to either side of a 4½" print square. **Make 1 row** like this. **6B**

Sew the 3 rows together to complete 1 shoofly block. **Make 12. 6C**

Block size: 12" finished

7 arrange and sew

Sew the blocks together into **5 rows** of **5 blocks**. The 54-40 or Fight blocks alternate with the Shoo Fly blocks. Notice that rows 1, 3, and 5 begin and end with a 54-40 or Fight block. Rows 2 and 4 begin and end with a Shoo Fly block. Sew the blocks into rows and press the seam allowances of the odd rows toward the left and the even rows toward the right. This helps the seams "nest."

Sew the rows together to complete the center of the quilt.

8 inner border

Cut (7) 2½" strips across the width of the fabric. Sew the strips together end-to-end to make one long strip. Trim the borders from this strip.

Refer to Borders (pg. 102) in the Construction Basics to measure and cut the inner borders. The strips are approximately 60½" for the sides and approximately 64½" for the top and bottom.

9 outer border

Cut (8) 6" strips across the width of the fabric. Sew the strips together end-to-end to make one long strip. Trim the borders from this strip.

Refer to Borders (pg. 102) in the Construction Basics to measure and cut the outer borders. The strips are approximately 64½" for the sides and approximately 75½" for the top and bottom.

10 quilt and bind

Layer the quilt with batting and backing and quilt. After the quilting is complete, square up the quilt and trim away all excess batting and backing. Add binding to complete the quilt. See Construction Basics (pg. 102) for binding instructions.

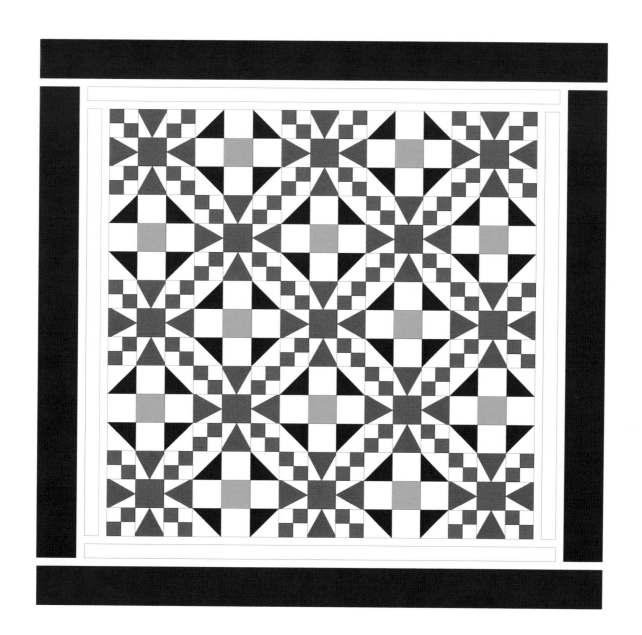

summer camp

For the tutorial and everything you need to make this quilt visit.
www.msqc.co/blockfall18

One hundred years ago, the world was a much quieter place. There were no televisions, no cell phones, and no digital distractions. Daily life provided plenty of opportunity for stillness and reflection. Not so today.

For the younger generations, they have no memory of life unplugged. My good friend Anna was so troubled at the constant blare of outside noise that always bombarded her grandchildren, she decided to take them to one place she had always found peace and quiet: into the woods.

When Anna's father was a young man, he had journeyed to a remote corner of the beautifully wild Uinta Mountains to assist a volunteer crew in constructing a youth camp for girls. All summer long, they hammered away in the shadow of lodgepole pines and quaking aspens, and before the first snowfall, they had completed ten small, bunk-filled cabins and one large A-frame lodge with floor-to-ceiling windows that faced the sparkling lake. Generations of girls - including a teen-aged Anna—had built happy memories paddling canoes, exploring quiet trails, and singing silly campfire songs under the light of a million sparkling stars. This was the kind of experience Anna wanted for her grandchildren.

Anna contacted the caretaker of the camp, and sure enough, there was an date available for the entire family to spend

the weekend at Grandpa's old lodge at the very tail end of the summer. So, they packed their bags and headed up to beautiful Lyman Lake.

That first day was magical—they raced canoes and hiked all the way around the lake. They discovered a beaver dam and watched chubby-cheeked chipmunks scamper along fallen logs. They roasted hotdogs over a crackling fire and Anna told her father's favorite old ghost story, The Wendigo. Then the parents carried their young children off to sleep in the small cabins that were scattered among the trees, while Anna and the older grandchildren climbed the steps to the top of the big, old lodge to spend the night in the bunk-filled loft.

The next morning, as they sat in the lodge feasting on hot pancakes and maple syrup, the sky grew dark and ominous. Suddenly, the heavens opened and rain came down in thick, silver sheets that pounded like thunder on the roof. Luckily, a little bit of rain couldn't keep this lot from having fun.

They pulled out card games. They played hide and seek. The kids learned how to build a fire in the big, open fireplace on the ground floor. They giggled, reminisced and had a wonderful time all together in that big, cozy lodge.

All through the weekend, rain or shine, they created memories of joyful, undistracted togetherness. No pressing emails. No breaking news. No texts or notifications or video games. It was just a grandmother and her sweet grandbabies, having the time of their lives.

materials

QUILT SIZE
62" X 78"

BLOCK SIZE
8" finished

QUILT TOP
1 roll of 2½" print strips
1¼ yards background fabric – includes
  inner border
¾ yard complementary solid fabric

OUTER BORDER
1¼ yards

BINDING
¾ yard

BACKING
4¾ yards - vertical seam(s)

SAMPLE QUILT
Road Trip by Alison Glass for Andover
Fabrics

1 cut

From the background fabric, cut:

- (2) 10" strips across the width
  of the fabric – subcut each strip
  into 10" squares. Each strip will
  yield 4 squares and a **total of 6**
  are needed. You will have 2
  squares left over for another
  project.

Set the remainder of the fabric aside for
the inner border.

From the complementary solid
fabric, cut:

- (2) 10" strips across the width
  of the fabric – subcut each strip
  into 10" squares. Each strip will

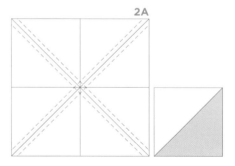

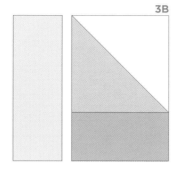

3B

3C

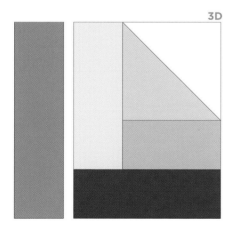

3D

yield 4 squares and a **total of 6** are needed. You will have 2 squares left over for another project.

From the roll of 2½" print strips, cut:

- 6 strips into 2½" x 4½" rectangles. Each strip will yield 8 rectangles and a **total of 48** are needed.

- 16 strips into 2½" x 6½" rectangles. Each strip will yield 6 rectangles and a **total of 96** are needed.

- 12 strips into 2½" x 8½" rectangles. Each strip will yield 4 rectangles and a **total of 48** are needed.

2 make half-square triangle units

Draw a line from corner to corner twice on the diagonal on the reverse side of each of the 10" background squares. Layer a marked background square with a solid square with right sides facing. Sew on both sides of the drawn lines using a ¼" seam allowance. Cut the sewn squares in half vertically and horizontally. Then cut on the drawn lines. Open each unit and press the seam allowance toward the darker fabric. Square each half-square triangle unit to 4½". **2A**

Each set of sewn squares will yield 8 half-square triangle units and a **total of 48** are needed.

3 block construction

Sew a 2½" x 4½" print rectangle to a half-square triangle unit. Make sure the rectangle is touching the solid color of the half-square triangle. **3A**

Add a 2½" x 6½" rectangle to the side. The rectangle should be touching the solid portion of the half-square triangle. **3B**

Add a 2½" x 6½" rectangle as shown. **3C**

Add a 2½" x 8½" rectangle to the side to complete the block. **Make 48. 3D**

Block Size: 8" finished

4 arrange and sew

Lay out the blocks in rows with each row made up of **6 blocks**. Make **8 rows**. Refer to the diagram on page 23 for placement. Take careful note of how each block is turned as you lay them out.

When you are satisfied with the arrangement, sew the blocks into rows. Press the odd-numbered rows toward the right and the even-numbered rows toward the left to make the seams "nest." Sew the rows together to complete the center of the quilt.

5 inner border

Cut (6) 2½" strips across the width of the fabric. Sew the strips together end-

1 Draw a line from corner to corner twice on the diagonal of each 10″ background square. Layer a background square with a print square with right sides facing. Sew on both sides of the drawn line using a ¼″ seam allowance. Cut the sewn squares in half horizontally and vertically, then cut on the drawn line.

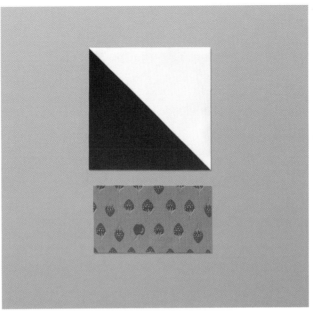

2 Sew a 2½″ x 4½″ print rectangle to the bottom of a half-square triangle unit.

3 Add a 2½″ x 6½″ print rectangle to the side as shown.

4 Sew a 2½″ x 6½″ print rectangle to the bottom of the unit.

5 Add a 2½″ x 8½″ print rectangle to the side to complete the block.

6 Make 48 blocks.

to-end to make one long strip. Trim the borders from this strip.

Refer to Borders (pg. 102) in the Construction Basics to measure and cut the inner borders. The strips are approximately 64½" for the sides and approximately 52½" for the top and bottom.

6 outer border

Cut (7) 5½" strips across the width of the fabric. Sew the strips together end-to-end to make one long strip. Trim the borders from this strip.

Refer to Borders (pg. 102) in the Construction Basics to measure and cut the outer borders. The strips are approximately 68½" for the sides and approximately 62½" for the top and bottom.

7 quilt and bind

Layer the quilt with batting and backing and quilt. After the quilting is complete, square up the quilt and trim away all excess batting and backing. Add binding to complete the quilt. See Construction Basics (pg. 102) for binding instructions.

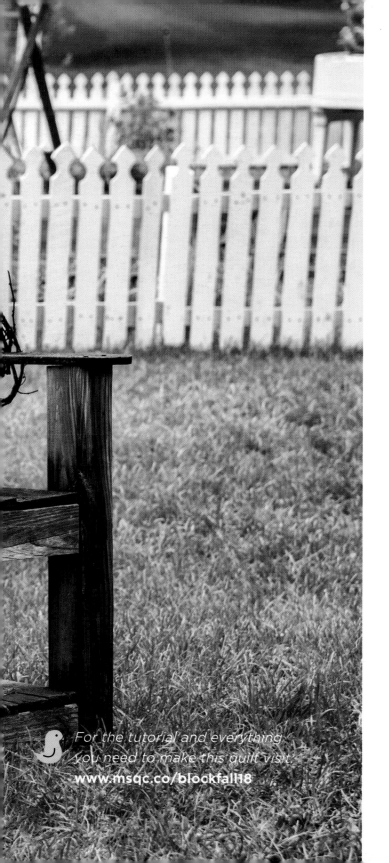

For the tutorial and everything you need to make this quilt visit:
www.msqc.co/blockfall18

royal
wedding

Squirrels and chipmunks love my yard. Last winter when an ice storm came through town, Ron and I watched as a little squirrel struggled to cross an icy telephone wire and it turned into a comedy of errors. As he sped up to stay on top of the wire, he quickly lost control and crash-landed into the side of the house! Poor thing. We got a good laugh watching his antics and if we'd had a video camera, we're sure that video could have won the $100,000 prize on America's Funniest Home Videos.

These lively rodents might be seen as bothersome, but they're actually pretty useful creatures. At the turn of last century, they were introduced into parks across the U.S. to create a more charming, entertaining atmosphere. In addition to this, they are wonderful helpers and each year they accidentally plant thousands of trees, simply by forgetting where they buried seeds and acorns!

My dad worked for Smucker's when I was a young girl and every now and then he would go on fruit-buying trips. During his excursions, he would often find interesting animals and bring them home for me, like a horned toad, a dog, or a bird. I would

25

wait for him to come back home with great anticipation, wondering what creature he might bring me. Once, my dad brought me home the cutest, tiny chipmunk, and he was one of my favorites. With his little whiskers and fuzzy tail, I couldn't help but adore him.

Playing with this chipmunk was a blast, at first. I'd let him out of his cage and he'd run around my room, rooting through piles of clothes and running across my bed, I had a darling yo-yo quilt on top of my bed, and he would weave in and out of it as quick as can be. It was tough to catch him, and I recall making a swift grab for

him and getting a bite in return. It wasn't pleasant, but my chipmunk lived to see another day, even though I entertained the idea of giving him away for such a nip!

Eventually the time came when I had to say goodbye to my chipmunk. As a child, it's a tough lesson to learn that animals don't live as long as we do, especially little chipmunks. I missed my chipmunk dearly, as you can imagine. Looking back, I'm not sure a pet chipmunk is the best idea (for child or chipmunk) but I am grateful for my adventurous father and the time I was able to spend taking care of such an interesting variety of pets. It helped me to be curious and more compassionate.

materials

QUILT SIZE
69" x 69"

BLOCK SIZE
18" finished

QUILT TOP
1 package of 10" print squares
½ yard white

BORDER
2 yards - includes sashing strips
and block pieces

BINDING
¾ yard

BACKING
4¼ yards - vertical seam(s)

SAMPLE QUILT
Wild Bouquet by Citrus and Mint
Designs for RIley Blake Designs

1 cut

From the border fabric, cut:

- (3) 4½" strips across the width of
  the fabric

- (3) 2½" strips across the width of the
  fabric – subcut the strips into 2½" x
  18½" rectangles. Each strip will yield
  2 rectangles and a **total of 6** are
  needed. Set aside to use for vertical
  sashing rectangles.

- (3) 2½" strips across the width of
  the fabric – set aside. We'll be using
  these strips to make our horizontal
  sashing strips.

Set aside the remaining fabric for the
border.

From the white fabric, cut:

- (3) 4½" strips across the width of
  the fabric.

- (1) 2½" strip across the width of the
  fabric – subcut (9) 2½" squares from
  the strip

2 make strip set

Sew a 4½" white strip to a 4½" strip cut
from the border fabric along the length
with right sides facing. Open and press
the seam allowance toward the darker
fabric. Make 3 and cut 2 strip sets into
2½" increments. Each strip set will yield
(16) 8½" rectangles. Cut 4 from the last
strip set. A **total of 36** are needed. **2A**

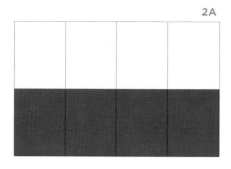

2A

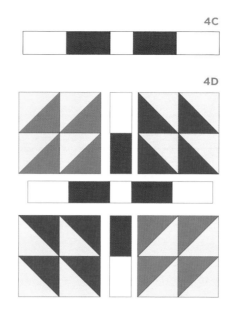

4C

4D

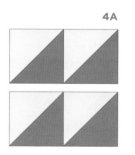

3A

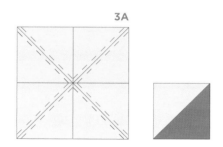

4A

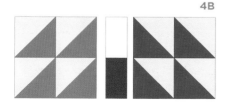

4B

4 block construction

Select 2 stacks of matching half-square triangles. Sew 4 half-square triangles into a 4-patch as shown. **Make 2.** Repeat for the remaining stack. **4A**

Make the top and bottom row of the block by sewing a 4-patch section to either side of a 2½" x 8½" strip set rectangle. **4B**

Make the center row of the block by sewing a 2½" x 8½" strip set rectangle to either side of a white 2½" square. Notice the darker portion of the rectangle touches the white square. **4C**

Sew the 3 rows together as shown to complete the block. **Make 9 blocks. 4D Block Size:** 18" finished

5 lay out and sew

Lay out the blocks in **3 rows of 3**. When you are happy with the arrangement, sew the blocks into rows. Add a 2½" x 18½" sashing rectangle between each block. Press the seam allowances in the first and third rows toward the right and those in the center row toward the left to make the seams "nest."

Before sewing the rows together, you will need to make 2 horizontal sashing strips. Pick up the 3 strips you set aside for this purpose. Sew the strips together end-to-end. Measure a couple of rows of blocks, they should be about 58½". Cut 2 strips to that measurement.

3 sew

Select 18 of the lighter colored 10" squares from the package. Draw a line from corner to corner twice on the diagonal on the reverse side of each lighter square.

Layer a marked square with a darker square with right sides facing. Sew on both sides of the lines using a ¼" seam allowance. Cut the sewn squares through the center horizontally and vertically. Then cut on the drawn lines. Open each to reveal a half-square triangle unit. Each set of sewn squares will yield 8 units and a **total of 144** are needed. Square each to 4½" and stack all matching prints together. **3A**

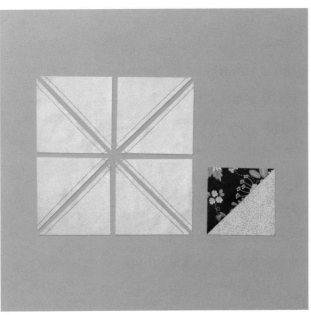

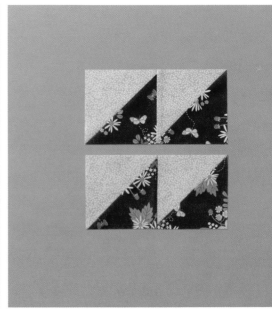

1 Sew a 4½" background strip to a 4½" strip that has been cut from the border fabric along the length with right sides facing. Open, press, and cut into 2½" increments.

2 Layer a marked lighter 10" square with a darker square with right sides facing. Sew on both sides of the lines using a ¼" seam allowance. Cut the sewn squares through the center horizontally and vertically. Then cut on the drawn line. Open, press and square each unit to 4½".

3 Select 2 sets of 4 matching half-square triangle units. Sew into a 4-patch formation. Make 2 from each set.

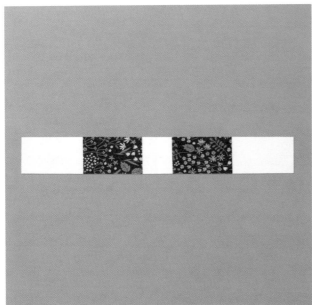

4 Make the center row of the block by sewing a 2½" x 8½" rectangle to either side of a background 2½" square.

5 Sew a 4-patch unit to either side of a 2½" x 8½" rectangle to make the top and bottom rows. Sew the 2 rows to a center row to complete the block. Notice that 2 contrasting sets of 4-patches were used.

Sew the rows together adding a horizontal sashing strip between the rows. Refer to the diagram on the left.

6 border

Cut (7) 6″ strips across the width of the fabric. Sew the strips together end-to-end to make one long strip. Trim the border pieces from this strip.

Refer to Borders (pg. 102) in the Construction Basics to measure and cut the borders. The strips are approximately 58½″ for the sides and approximately 69½″ for the top and bottom.

7 quilt and bind

Layer the quilt with batting and backing and quilt. After the quilting is complete, square up the quilt and trim away all excess batting and backing. Add binding to complete the quilt. See Construction Basics (pg. 102) for binding instructions

For the tutorial and everything
you need to make this quilt visit:
www.msqc.co/blockfall18

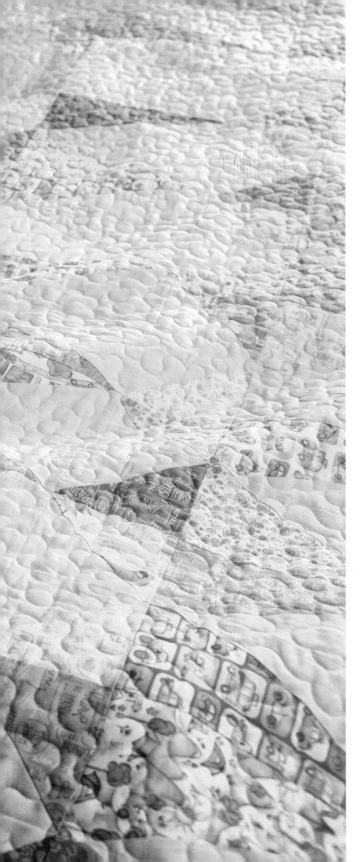

kite season

Chilly weather brings with it a host of sniffles and coughs. While there isn't a cure for the common cold, we're always on the hunt for any remedy that will bring a bit of relief.

When Maren was twenty-one years old, she traveled to St Petersburg, Russia, for eighteen months of frigid adventure. In the midst of a particularly bitter cold snap, Maren's roommate, Becky, came down with a terrible head cold.

Sweet old Russian grandmas, or babushkas, were eager to offer ancient healing recipes and folk remedies.

"Soak two cotton balls in onion juice and stick one up each nostril. That runny nose will be dried up in no time."

"Stir a spoonful of raspberry preserves into your tea. And don't forget a splash of vodka."

"Wear this string of garlic beads around your neck. You won't smell great, but it'll chase that cold right away."

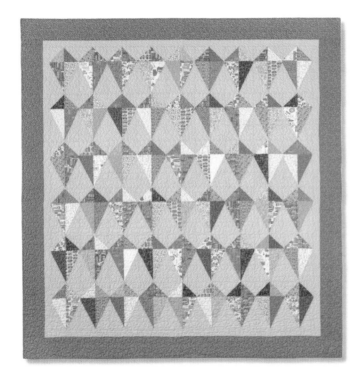

A well-meaning neighbor even taped a matchstick to each side of Becky's nose. And whether it was the matchsticks, the cupfulls of raspberry-jam tea, or just dumb luck, Becky felt better by the weekend.

Of course, Russia isn't the only place to find unique cures for the common cold. In China, you may be offered lizard soup. In England, you may be asked to slather chicken fat on your neck and wrap it with a dirty sock. And in the United States? Well, we have plenty of strange old remedies of our own. Here are a few of my favorites:

* Accidentally fall into a creek. (Yes, it must be an accident.)
* Place a toenail clipping in the hollow of a tree.
* Drink water from a stranger's shoe.
* Ask a long-time smoker to blow his breath down your throat.

Of course, an ounce of prevention is worth a pound of cure, so be sure to safeguard yourself from catching a cold with this wise, old American trick: Cut an onion in half, hang it by a string, and every time you pass by, give it a little "bop." It's as easy as that!

If these handy tips and tricks don't work for you, here's my best advice: Wrap up in your coziest quilt, cue up a favorite old movie, and get plenty of rest and relaxation. I'm sure you'll be feeling better in no time!

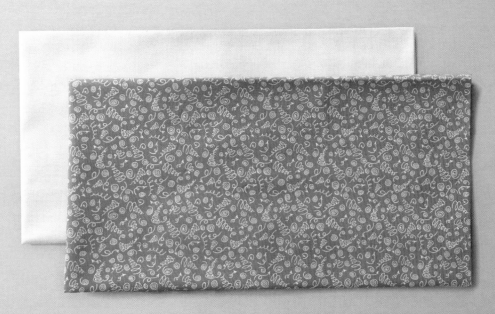
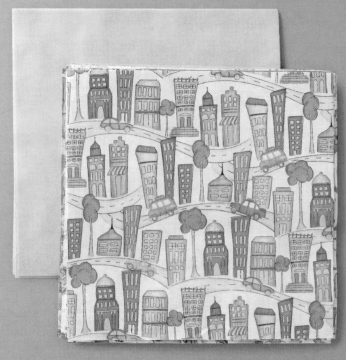

materials

QUILT SIZE
88" x 94"

BLOCK SIZE
8" x 13" finished

QUILT TOP
1 package of 10" print squares
3¾ yards of background fabric
 - includes inner border

BORDER
1¾ yards

BINDING
¾ yard

BACKING
8 yards - horizontal seam(s)
 - or 3 yards 108" wide

SAMPLE QUILT
Road Trippin by Terri Degenkolb for
Windham Fabrics

1 layer, cut, and sew

Cut (11) 10" strips across the width of
the fabric. Subcut each strip into 10"
squares. Each strip will yield 4 squares
and a total of **41 squares** are needed.

Set 1 square from the package of 10"
print squares aside for another project.

Layer a print square with a background
square. Cut the layered pieces in half
vertically making 5" x 10" rectangles
– subcut 27 layered rectangles in half
horizontally to make 5" squares for a
total of 54 print 5" squares and **54
background 5" squares.** Set aside all the
remaining rectangles for the moment. **1A**

1A

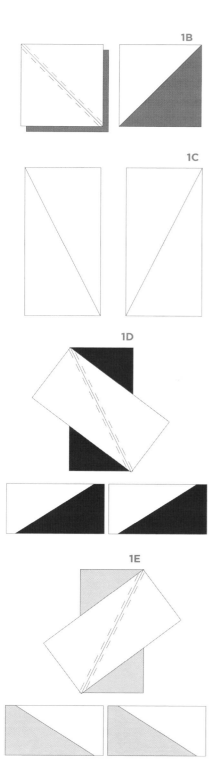

On the reverse side of each 5″ background square, draw a line from corner to corner once on the diagonal. Sew on both sides of the drawn line using a ¼″ seam allowance. Cut on the drawn line and open each side to reveal a half-square triangle unit. You will have a **total of 108 half-square triangles.** Square each to 4½″. **1B**

On the reverse side of 27 of the 5″ x 10″ background rectangles, draw a line from corner to corner once on the diagonal with the line going from the lower right corner to the upper left corner. On the reverse side of the 27 remaining 5″ x 10″ background rectangles, draw a line from corner to corner once on the diagonal with the line going from the lower left corner to the upper right corner. **1C**

Note: you will have 1 print and 1 background 5″ x 10″ rectangle left over for another project.

Place a marked background rectangle atop a print rectangle as shown with right sides facing. Notice that the marked line is running from the lower right to the upper left. Sew on both sides of the drawn line using a ¼″ seam allowance. Cut along the drawn line, open each to reveal 2 units. Press the seam allowance toward the darker fabric. You will have a **total of 54 units.** We'll call these unit A for clarity. **1D**

Place a marked background rectangle atop a print rectangle as shown with right sides facing. Notice that the marked

line is running from the lower left to the upper right. Sew on both sides of the drawn line using a ¼″ seam allowance. Cut along the drawn line, open each to reveal 2 units. Press the seam allowance toward the darker fabric. You will have a **total of 54 units.** We'll call these unit B. **1E**

2 block construction

Sew 2 half-square triangle units together as shown to make the top portion of the kite. **2A**

Sew Unit A to Unit B to make the bottom part of the kite. **2B**

Align the center seam allowance of the top portion of the kite with the center seam allowance of the bottom portion, then sew the two parts together to complete the block. **Make 54** and square each to 8½″ x 13½″. **2C**

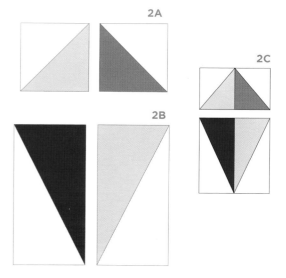

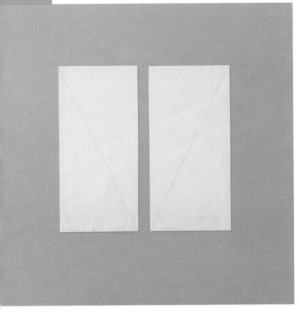

1 On the reverse side of 27 background rectangles, draw a line from corner to corner once on the diagonal with the line going from the lower right corner to the upper left. Draw a line from the lower left corner to the upper right on the reverse side of the remaining 27 background rectangles.

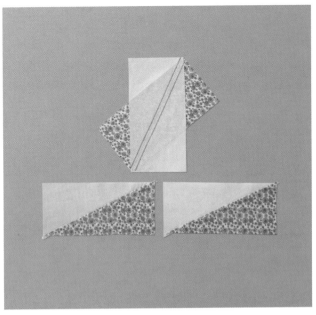

2 To make Unit A, place a marked background rectangle atop a print rectangle. Be aware of the orientation of the diagonal line. Sew on both sides of the drawn line using a ¼" seam allowance. Cut on the drawn line and open to reveal 2 half-rectangles.

3 To make Unit B, place a marked background rectangle atop a print rectangle. Be aware of the orientation of the diagonal line. Sew on both sides of the drawn line using a ¼" seam allowance. Cut on the drawn line and open to reveal 2 half-rectangles. Notice that Unit B is a mirror image of Unit A.

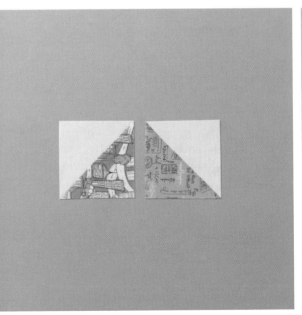

4 Sew 2 half-square triangle units together to make the top portion of the kite.

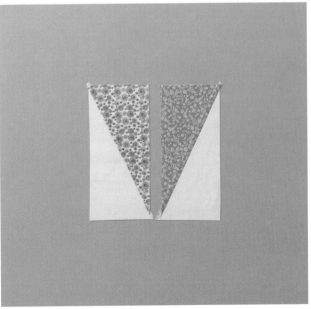

5 Sew Unit A to Unit B to make the bottom portion of the kite.

6 Sew the top portion of the kite to the bottom to complete the block.

3 arrange and sew

Lay out the blocks in rows. Each row is made up of **9 blocks** across. A **total of 6 rows** are needed.

Once the blocks are arranged to your satisfaction, sew them into rows. Press the seam allowances of the odd rows toward the right and those of the even rows toward the left to make the seam allowances "nest".

4 inner border

Cut (8) 2½" strips across the width of the fabric. Sew the strips together end-to-end to make one long strip. Trim the borders from this strip.

Refer to Borders (pg. 102) in the Construction Basics to measure and cut the inner borders. The strips are approximately 78½" for the sides and approximately 76½" for the top and bottom.

5 outer border

Cut (9) 6½" strips across the width of the fabric. Sew the strips together end-to-end to make one long strip. Trim the borders from this strip.

Refer to Borders (pg. 102) in the Construction Basics to measure and cut the outer borders. The strips are approximately 82½" for the sides and approximately 88½" for the top and bottom.

6 quilt and bind

Layer the quilt with batting and backing and quilt. After the quilting is complete, square up the quilt and trim away all excess batting and backing. Add binding to complete the quilt. See Construction Basics (pg. 102) for binding instructions.

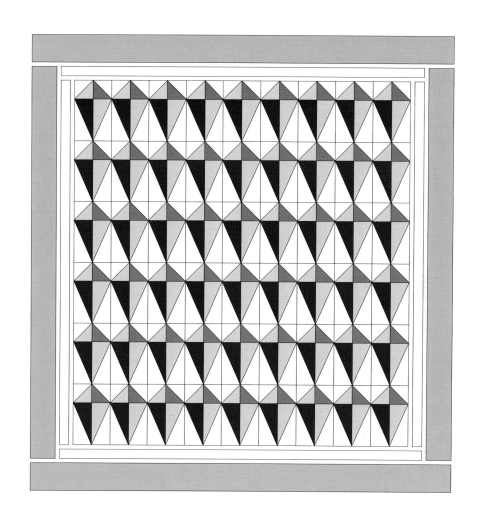

treasure
box

It wasn't officially fall yet; In fact, it was only September when Kristy and her sister, Kelly, stopped in at the most fragrant store in the mall: the soap and lotion store. The store had just released their line of pumpkin spice products, and Kristy, a confirmed pumpkin spice addict, wanted all of it! When the two sisters approached the front of the store, that tell-tale scent, along with the clamoring crowd that wanted it, was spilling right out into the mall. "Come on," Kristy said as she looped her arm through Kelly's, "we'll just have to squeeze our way through." And they did just that. Holding on tight to each other, the two brave sisters found a sliver of space within the pumpkin spice frenzy, and pushed their way through!

Once inside, the spicy sweet aroma became thicker, and the crowd became louder. Customers were shouting, dousing themselves in pumpkin spice perfumes, treating themselves to free exfoliating hand washes, and burying their noses in pumpkin spice latte candles. Just as Kelly was about to ask Kristy where she wanted to start first, she realized the crook of her arm was feeling very empty. Kelly looked to her right, and saw that she was suddenly sisterless! Kelly saw that the entrance was completely blocked off as more and more customers came filing in, so she decided to go deeper into the store to find Kristy.

For the tutorial and everything you need to make this quilt visit: www.msqc.co/blockfall18

41

Squeezing, bobbing, and weaving through the crazed crowd, Kelly spotted Kristy standing in front of a display that looked rather empty. "I can't believe you ditched me!" Kelly said as she approached her sister. When Kristy turned around, Kelly's jaw dropped to the floor, and she saw why the display was so bare. Her sister was all but hidden behind an orange mountain of pumpkin spice products! In her arms, Kristy was cradling pumpkin spice candles, perfumes, shower scrubs, shower gels, and lotions. Kristy strained to peer over her pile of pumpkin spice loot. "Hey, can you help me with this stuff?" She asked Kelly, who put her hands on her hips and shook her head. "Help? There is no help for you!" Still shaking her head, Kelly took a few items from her sister's trembling arms, and led her to the checkout line.

Once it was finally their turn and the cashier started ringing up the items, Kelly noticed her sister's wandering eye. "Don't even think about it!" Kelly scolded. Kristy had her eyes on a shiny, pumpkin-shaped night light, "But I kind of want…"

"That'll be $102.73, please," the cashier chimed. Kelly gasped, but Kristy handed her debit card over without batting an eyelash! After paying, Kristy and Kelly grabbed the two bulging bags of pumpkin spice goods and squeezed through the crowd one last time. Once out the store, Kelly breathed in deep. "Ah, fresh air!" Kristy was looking into one of her bags, admiring her new pumpkin spice scents.

"Congratulations, Kristy," Kelly began, "I'm pretty sure you just spent your electric bill money on pumpkin spice nonsense. What are you going to do next?"

"Get a pumpkin spice latte!"

materials

QUILT SIZE
39" x 44"

BLOCK SIZE
5" finished

QUILT TOP
1 package 5" print or solid squares
1 package 5" background squares

INNER BORDER
¼ yard

OUTER BORDER
½ yard

BINDING
½ yard

BACKING
3 yards - vertical seam(s)

SAMPLE QUILT
Top Drawer by Kathy Hall for
Andover Fabrics

1 sew

Layer a 5" print square with a 5"
background square with right sides
facing. Sew all the way around the outer
perimeter using a ¼" seam allowance.
Cut the sewn squares from corner to
corner twice on the diagonal. Open
each to reveal 4 half-square triangle
units. Keep all matching pieces stacked
together. You should have a **total of 168**
half-square triangle units. Square up each
unit to 3". **1A**

Pick up a stack of 4 matching half-square
triangles. Sew them together in a 4-patch
formation as shown to make Block A.

Make 24. 1B

1A

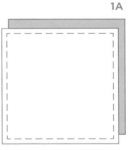

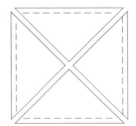

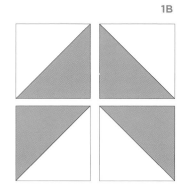

1B

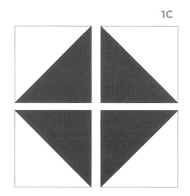

1C

Sew the remaining half-square triangles together into a 4-patch formation as shown to make Block B. **Make 18.** 1C

Block Sizes: 5″ finished

2 arrange and sew

Lay out the blocks in rows. Each row should have **6 blocks** across and you need a total of **7 rows.** Rows 1, 3, 5, and 7 are all made using Block A. Be aware of how the blocks are oriented as you arrange them into rows. Rows 2, 4, and 6 are made using Block B.

Once you have sewn the blocks into rows, press the seam allowances in the odd rows toward the right and the even rows toward the left so the seams will "nest."

Sew the rows together. Refer to the diagram on page 47 if necessary.

3 inner border

Cut (4) 1½″ strips across the width of the fabric. Trim the borders from these strips.

Refer to Borders (pg. 102) in the Construction Basics to measure and cut the inner borders. The strips are approximately 35½″ for the sides and approximately 32½″ for the top and bottom.

4 outer border

Cut (4) 4″ strips across the width of the fabric. Trim the borders from these strips.

Refer to Borders (pg. 102) in the Construction Basics to measure and cut the outer borders. The strips are approximately 37½″ for the sides and approximately 39½″ for the top and bottom.

5 quilt and bind

Layer the quilt with batting and backing and quilt. After the quilting is complete, square up the quilt and trim away all excess batting and backing. Add binding to complete the quilt. See Construction Basics (pg. 102) for binding instructions.

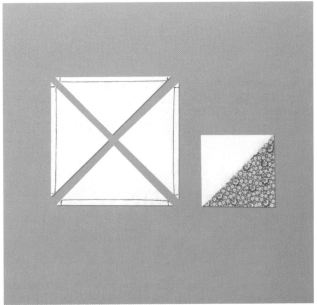

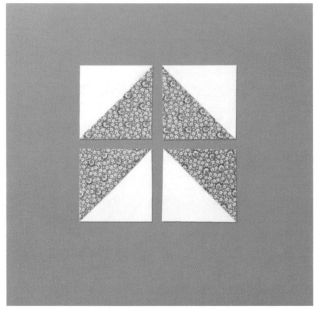

1   Layer a 5″ print square with a 5″ background square with right sides facing. Sew around the outer perimeter using a ¼″ seam allowance. Cut the sewn squares twice on the diagonal. Open each to reveal a half-square triangle unit.

2   Select 4 matching half-square triangles. Sew them together in a 4-patch formation as shown to make Block A.

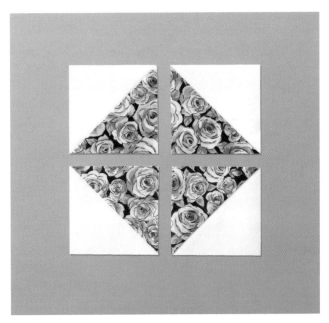

3   Select 4 matching half-square triangles. Sew them together in a 4-patch formation to make Block B.

jitterbug

Recently I was driving down the road, and I saw a bumper sticker that said, "If you can read this, thank a teacher." It made me think back on those early years of learning and the importance of all of my teachers struck me in that moment. Teachers play such an important role in our world. We are surrounded by teachers all our lives, whether they are formal classroom teachers, parents, friends, grandparents, or mentors, and our lives wouldn't be the same without them. We are shaped by these kind individuals who are patient with us as we seek to understand the world.

In 1971, I was a freshman at Salinas High School. Go Cowboys! It was a beautiful old high school that mirrored the architecture of the old missions along the California coast. I was the first girl in my high school to take shop, and when I was a freshman, women were finally allowed to wear pants on campus one day a week. I was also in choir, and it was a sweet, safe place for me for all four years of my high school experience. I was so grateful to be a part of the choir. Practically everyone tried out, but there were few freshmen chosen and I couldn't believe how lucky I was.

During those years, I had many wonderful teachers, but one of my favorites was a man named Mr. Green. There are certain teachers who can pull more out of you than you ever knew

For the tutorial and everything you need to make this quilt visit: **www.msqc.co/blockfall18**

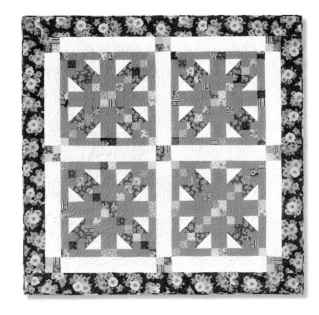

you could give and that was how he was. Mr. Green was my high school choir teacher and I became a better singer because of him. He expected excellence from us, but he was never impatient or judgmental. It was about perseverance. All his instruction was focused on helping us to believe in our abilities and dig deeper than we previously believed we could. As a result, we often learned music we didn't know we were capable of learning. It was incredible to be a part of that choir and sing together in such a powerful way. I loved that moment when, all of a sudden, the music would end and while the beautiful reverberations were echoing through the stillness, I would get goosebumps.

Another thing I admired about Mr. Green was how he helped us to realize that it took all of us. We had to work together. We were singing intricate parts. One person can't make a choir. When everyone does their part well, you make something that wasn't there before. He also taught us how much hard work pays off and how important it is to have everyone do their best. He was a teacher that the students could really relate to, and he helped shape my life. I didn't know what my potential was until Mr. Green came along and helped me realize what I could do.

So, when you get a spare moment, think about a teacher or a mentor in your life and be sure to tell them thank you! Their jobs aren't easy, and they may not see the fruits of their labors for years. Seeing a student's eyes light up as they begin to make connections is well worth their tireless efforts. You are the reason they do what they do.

materials

QUILT SIZE
71″ X 71″

BLOCK SIZE
24″ finished

QUILT TOP
1 package 5″ squares
1½ yards medium blue solid
2 yards white
½ yard medium blue print

BORDER
1¼ yards

BINDING
¾ yard

BACKING
4½ yards - vertical seam(s)

SAMPLE QUILT
Garden Side Path by Rebecca Baer
for Robert Kaufman Fabrics

1 cut

Cut each of (41) 5″ squares in half vertically and horizontally. Each square will yield (4) 2½″ squares and a **total of 164** are needed. You will have (1) 5″ square left over.

From the medium blue fabric, cut:

- (20) 2½″ strips across the width of the fabric – subcut 16 strips into 2½″ x 4½″ rectangles. Each strip will yield 8 rectangles and a **total of 128** are needed.
  Cut the remaining 4 strips into 2½″ squares. Each strip will yield 16 squares and you need a **total of 64.**

From the white fabric, cut:

- (2) 5″ strips across the width of the fabric – subcut each strip into 5″ squares. Each strip will yield 8 squares and a **total of 16** are needed.

- (12) 4½″ strips across the width of the fabric – subcut each strip into (1) 4½″ x 24½″ rectangle. A **total of 12 rectangles** are needed. Set them aside for the sashing strips.

From the medium blue print fabric, cut:

- (2) 5″ strips across the width of the fabric – subcut each strip into 5″ squares. Each strip will yield 8 squares and a **total of 16** are needed.

2 sew

Each block uses 2 different units.

unit a

Sew a 2½" medium blue square to a print square. **Make 2** and sew them into a 4-patch formation. **2A**

Sew a medium blue 2½" x 4½" strip to one side of the 4-patch. **2B**

Sew a 2½" print square to one end of a 2½" x 4½" medium blue rectangle. **2C**

Add the pieced rectangle to complete the unit. **Make 8** for each block. A **total of 32** are needed for the whole quilt. **2D**

unit b

Draw a line from corner to corner once on the diagonal on the reverse side of a white 5" square. Layer a white 5" square with a medium blue print 5" square with right sides facing. Sew on both sides of the drawn line using a ¼" seam allowance. Cut on the drawn line. Open each side to reveal a half-square triangle. Press the seam allowance toward the darker fabric, then square each to 4½". Each square will yield 2 half-square triangles and **each block uses 8**. **2E**

Sew a 2½" x 4½" medium blue rectangle to a half-square triangle. Notice that the rectangle is touching the white portion of the half-square triangle. **2F**

Sew a 2½" print square to one end of a 2½" x 4½" medium blue rectangle. **2G**

53

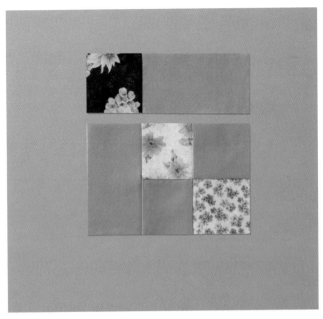

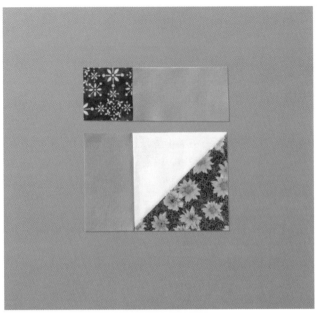

1   Sew 4 squares together in a 4-patch formation. Add a 2½" x 4½" rectangle to one side of the 4-patch. Sew a 2½" print square to a 2½" x 4½" rectangle and sew it to the top to make Unit A. Make 8 per block.

2   Sew a 2½" x 4½" rectangle to a half-square triangle as shown. Stitch a 2½" print square to a 2½" x 4½" rectangle. Sew it to the top to make unit B. Make 8 per block.

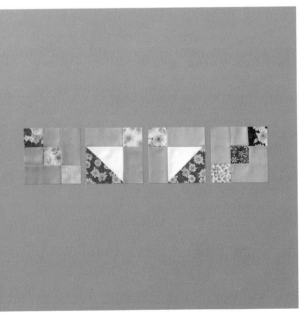

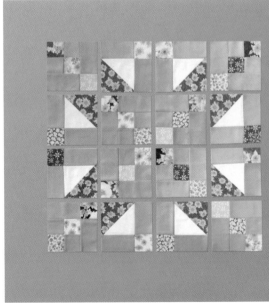

3   Make rows 1 and 4 by sewing Unit A to Unit B. Follow with Unit B and add another Unit A. Be aware of how each unit is oriented.

4   Make rows 2 and 3 by sewing Unit B to Unit A. Add another Unit A and end the row with a Unit B.

5   Sew the 4 rows together to complete 1 block. Make 4.

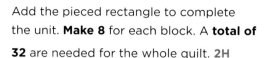

4B

Add the pieced rectangle to complete the unit. **Make 8** for each block. A **total of 32** are needed for the whole quilt. **2H**

3 block construction

Make a row by sewing Unit A to Unit B. Follow with another Unit B and end the row by joining a Unit A. **Make 2 rows** like this. **3A**

Sew a Unit B to a Unit A. Add another Unit A and end the row with a Unit B. **Make 2 rows** like this. **3B**

Sew the 4 rows together to complete the block. **3C**

Make 4 blocks.

Block size: 24″ finished

4 arrange and sew

Lay out the blocks in rows. Each row is made up of **2 blocks** and **2 rows** are needed. Sew a 4½″ x 24½″ sashing rectangle between each block and at the end of each row. Press the sashing toward the blocks.

Make horizontal sashing rows. Begin by making 4-patch units. Sew (4) 2½″ squares together as shown to make a 4-patch unit. **Make 9. 4A**

Sew a 4-patch unit to a white 4½″ x 24½″ rectangle. Add a 4-patch, then another 4½″ x 24½″ rectangle. Finish the row by adding a 4-patch unit. Press the seams toward the 4-patch units. **Make 3 rows** in this manner. **4B**

Sew the rows together and add a horizontal sashing row between the two rows. Add a horizontal sashing row to the top and bottom of the quilt top to complete the center of the quilt.

5 border

Cut (7) 6″ strips across the width of the fabric. Sew the strips together end-to-end to make one long strip. Trim the borders from this strip.

Refer to Borders (pg. 102) in the Construction Basics to measure and cut the outer borders. The strips are approximately 60½″ for the sides and approximately 71½″ for the top and bottom.

6 quilt and bind

Layer the quilt with batting and backing and quilt. After the quilting is complete, square up the quilt and trim away all excess batting and backing. Add binding to complete the quilt. See Construction Basics (pg. 102) for binding instructions.

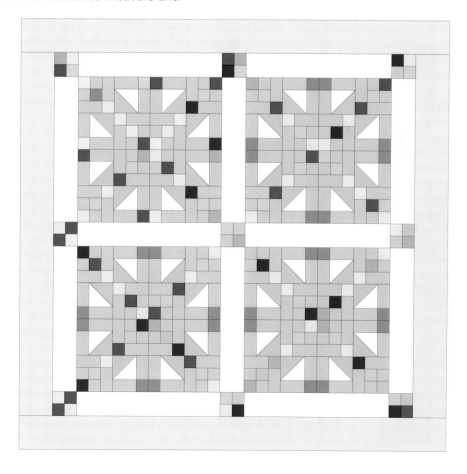

For the tutorial and everything you need to make this quilt visit:
www.msqc.co/blockfall18

jenny's
doll quilt

It's one of the great miracles of nature: A tiny white blossom pops up on a winter-bare branch. Day by day, it grows and matures into a big, juicy pear just waiting to be eaten. The only trouble is that pear is accompanied by hundreds of its brothers and sisters.

Wouldn't it be lovely if pears ripened only a few at a time? Every day at noon you could wander out to the tree and grab one perfect pear to enjoy with lunch. But, alas, when the pears are ready, they're ready all at once. So you have two choices: stuff yourself with freshly-picked pears and let the rest go to waste, or get to work and can 'em!

When Ellie Lawrence was growing up, early autumn was always canning time. From the moment the fruit was ready to be picked, all other activities were put on hold until the very last pear had been carefully preserved.

Ellie's Grandma Afton always arrived at the house early in the morning with boxes of empty quart jars and lids. Mom, Dad, Ellie, and her two older sisters sat around the kitchen table, each of them outfitted with a small knife and a pan for peelings as Grandma prepared clean jars with an inch or two of water and sugar.

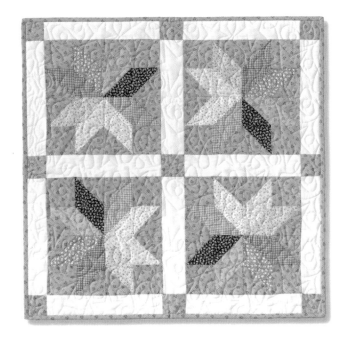

One by one, the pears were peeled, sliced in half, and cored before being placed in the jars. Grandma was a blue-ribbon canner who had spent years judging at the county fair, and she oversaw the entire process with a great deal of care. The pears had to be carefully nested so that only the smooth, round side of each pear half showed. "You can fit more pears that way. Besides, if a judge ever spotted a single pear turned the other way, that'd be a white ribbon for sure!"

After the jars were filled, Grandma placed a lid on each one and fastened it tight with a screw-on ring. Then they were lowered into a large pot of boiling water to process while the crew took a break for a lunch.

When the timer buzzed, Ellie always begged to be the one to remove the jars from the water. Grandma had a special tool that grabbed the jars like a funny-shaped pair of tongs. Ellie lifted each jar with care and set them on towels that had been spread out on the countertop. One by one, the cooling jars would produce a little "pop" as the lids sealed.

When every jar had been sealed and inspected, they were carried down to the cellar shelves and carefully arranged in neat rows next to dozens of jars of green beans, grape juice, stewed tomatoes, homemade salsa, and five different types of jam.

It was an awful lot of work, but looking at all that carefully stored food, Ellie felt an overwhelming sense of gratitude for the blessing of an abundant harvest that would last all winter long.

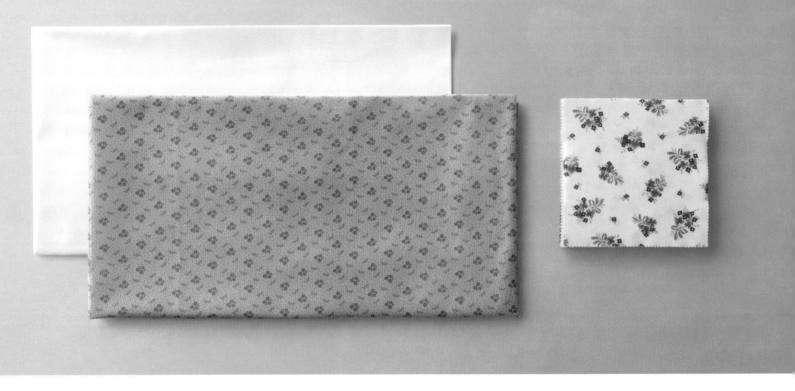

materials

QUILT SIZE
26″ x 26″

BLOCK SIZE
10″ finished

QUILT TOP
1 package of 5″ print squares
½ yard background fabric
  - includes cornerstones
½ yard white solid

BINDING
½ yard

BACKING
1 yard

SAMPLE QUILT
Guest Room by Kristyne Czepuryk
of Pretty by Hand for Moda Fabrics

1 cut

From the background fabric, cut:

- (1) 5″ strip across the width of the fabric – subcut the strip into (8) 5″ squares.

- (2) 3″ strips across the width of the fabric – subcut each strip into 3″ squares. Each strip will yield 13 squares and a **total of 16** are needed for the blocks. There will be 10 squares left over. Trim 9 of these squares to 2½″ and set aside to use as cornerstones in the sashing/borders.

From the white solid, cut:

- (3) 2½″ strips across the width of the fabric - subcut each strip into 2½″ x 10½″ rectangles. Each strip will yield 4 rectangles and a **total of 12** are needed. Set aside to use as sashing rectangles.

2 sew

Select 8 pairs of matching 5″ print squares. Set 4 pairs aside for the moment. Place a 5″ background square atop a print square with right sides facing. Sew around the perimeter of the square ¼″ from the edge. Cut the stitched squares from corner to corner twice on the diagonal. Open to reveal 4 matching half-square triangles. Press the seam allowance toward the darker fabric. Repeat, pairing a background square with a 5″ print square, each time using a different print. You'll have a **total of 32 half-square triangles.** Square each to 3″. **2A**

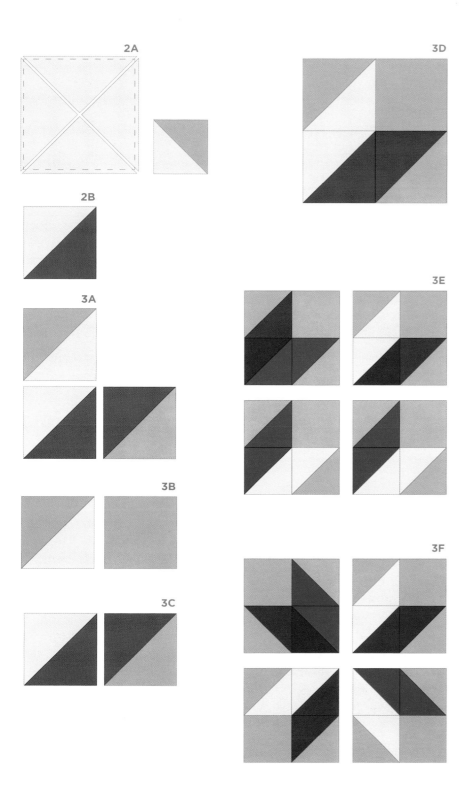

Using the print squares you set aside, make 4 matching half-square triangles by pairing 2 contrasting prints. Repeat, using the remaining print squares from the pairs. You will have a **total of 16 half-square triangles.** Square each to 3". **2B**

3 block construction

Lay out a print/print half-square triangle unit. Pick up print/background units that match the prints used. Lay them out as they will be sewn together so you can keep all matching prints together. **3A**

Sew a 3" background square to the right of the half-square triangle that is placed at the top of the print/print half-square triangle. **3B**

Sew a background/print half-square triangle unit that uses a matching print to the right of the print/print half-square triangle unit as shown. **3C**

Sew the two rows you have just made together. This makes up one quadrant of one block. Make 4 exactly alike. **3D**

Repeat the above instructions and make quadrants by using matching half-square triangle units as before. You should have 4 sets of 4. **3E**

Sew 4 quadrants together as shown to create 1 block. Make **4 blocks**. **3F**

Note: all blocks are made exactly alike.
Block Size: 10" finished

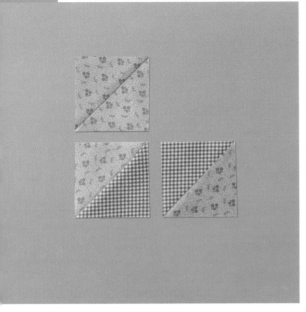

1 Lay out a print/print half-square triangle unit. Pick up print/background units that match the prints used. Lay them out as they will be sewn together so you can keep all matching prints together.

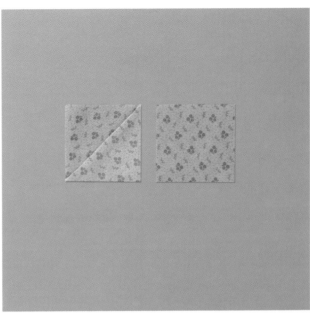

2 Sew a 3″ background square to the right of the half-square triangle that is placed at the top of the print/print half-square triangle unit.

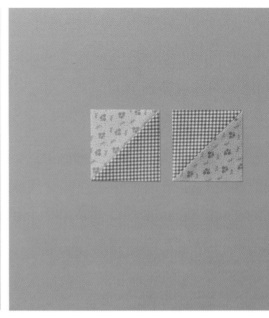

3 Sew a background/print half-square triangle that uses a matching print to the right of the print/print half-square triangle unit as shown.

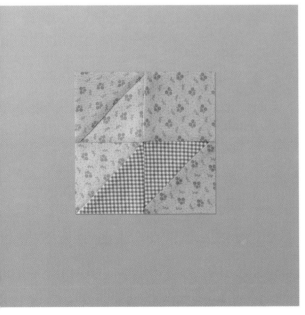

4 Sew the 2 rows you have just made into a 4-patch formation.

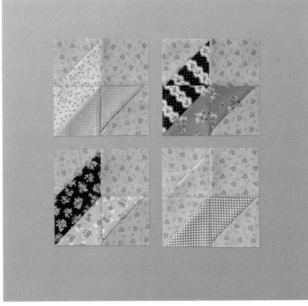

5 Make 4 quadrants by using the matching half-square triangle units as before. You should have 4 sets of 4.

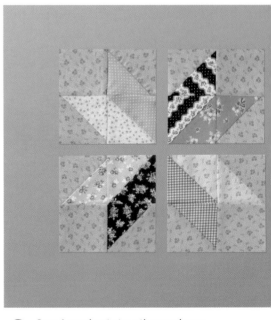

6 Sew 4 quadrants together as shown to complete the block. Make 4.

4 arrange and sew

Arrange the 4 blocks into **2 rows** with each row having **2 blocks**. Notice as the blocks are placed, each has been turned one-quarter turn. Sew a 2½" x 10½" sashing rectangle between each block and on each end.

Make 3 horizontal sashing strips by sewing a 2½" cornerstone to a sashing rectangle. Add a cornerstone, another rectangle and end the row with a cornerstone. **Make 3.**

Sew the rows and the horizontal sashing strips together to complete the quilt. Refer to the diagram on the left for placement.

5 quilt and bind

Layer the quilt with batting and backing and quilt. After the quilting is complete, square up the quilt and trim away all excess batting and backing. Add binding to complete the quilt. See Construction Basics (pg. 102) for binding instructions

north *star*

Thanksgiving is just around the corner, so let's talk turkey! Standing in the grocery aisle and gazing upon the endless heaps of frozen turkeys gives us little perspective about why they are the center of our feast. Of course they're tasty, but what makes turkeys so special?

First of all, of the few things we eat that may have actually been at the original Thanksgiving dinner, the turkey was most definitely present. This bird has been around for quite a long time. Native to North America, both the Pilgrims and Native Americans hunted and ate Eastern wild turkey.

But there was a time when turkeys were endangered. In the early 1900s, only about 30,000 turkeys remained in the wild. Thankfully, great care has been taken to restore their numbers since that time, and today there are more than seven million thriving all over the world. After all, what would Thanksgiving be without them?

You may have also heard that the turkey was almost our national bird. Well, that's not exactly true. Benjamin Franklin said about the choice of the bald eagle: "The turkey is in comparison a much more respectable bird, and withal a true original native of America... He is besides, though a little vain and silly, a bird of courage." He believed the turkey to be a better representation of our values, but the turkey was never seriously considered.

Despite being overlooked as a candidate for our national bird, turkeys are pretty terrific. When I was a child, we sang a song in school about turkeys, and it makes me smile every time I hear it. The lyrics seem to

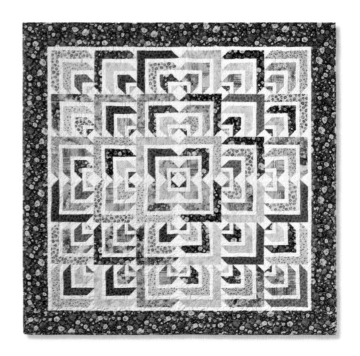

be a bit different depending on who you ask, but this is what I learned when I was little:

There's a big, fat turkey on Grandpa's farm
And he thinks he's really great.
He spreads his tail into a great, big fan
And he struts around all day.

You can hear him gobble at the girls and boys,
For he thinks he's singing when he makes that noise,
But he'll sing his song another way
Upon Thanksgiving Day!

materials

QUILT SIZE
80" x 80"

BLOCK SIZE
11" finished

QUILT TOP
1 roll 1½" white strips - includes inner
  border
1 roll 2½" print strips
3 packages of 2½" squares - 84 count

BORDER
1¾ yards

BINDING
¾ yard

BACKING
7½ yards - vertical seam(s)
  or 2½ yards 108" wide

SAMPLE QUILT
Petal Park by RJR Fabrics

1 cut

Set aside (7) 1½" white strips for the border.

From the remaining 1½" white strips, cut:

- 9 strips into (4) 1½" x 9½" rectangles and (1) 1½" x 2½" rectangle. Each strip will yield 4 large rectangles for a **total of 36** and 1 small rectangle for a **total of 9.** Set the small rectangles aside for the moment. We'll be adding to the stack.

- 9 strips into (4) 1½" x 8½" rectangles and (3) 1½" x 2½" rectangles. You will have a total of 36 large rectangles and 27 small rectangles. Stack these with the 9 rectangles cut previously. You should have a **total of 36.**

- 6 strips into 1½" x 6½" rectangles. Each strip will yield 6 rectangles and a **total of 36** are needed

- 6 strips – cut 5 strips into (7) 1½" x 5½" rectangles for a **total of 35** and (1) 1½" x 5½" rectangle from the remaining strip. Set aside the remaining piece. We'll be using it up for other sizes.

- 3 strips into 1½" x 3½" rectangles. Each strip will yield 11 rectangles and a **total of 36** are needed. Pick up the leftover piece you have after cutting the 5½" rectangles. From that piece, cut (3) 1½" x 3½" rectangles and add them to the stack of 33 you've just cut.

From the border fabric, cut:

- (2) 2½" strips and add them to the roll of print 2½" strips.

From the 2½" print strips:

Select 18 strips and cut:

- (2) 11½" rectangles and (2) 9½" rectangles from each strip for a **total of 36** of each size of rectangle. Stack all matching prints together.

Select 18 strips and cut:

- (2) 8½" rectangles, (2) 6½" rectangles, (1) 5½" rectangle, (1) 3½" rectangle, (1) 2½" square from each strip. You will have a **total of (36)** 8½" rectangles and (36) 6½" rectangles as well as 18 rectangles of each of the remaining sizes. Stack all matching prints together.

From 5 of the remaining strips, cut:

- (4) 5½" rectangles, (4) 3½" rectangles and (2) 2½" squares from each strip. You will have a **total of 20** of each size rectangles and 10 squares. Add those to the 18 pieces you have already cut. You need a **total of 36** of each size rectangle and of the 2½" squares as well. Stack all matching prints together.

From the last 2½" print strip, cut:

- (8) 2½" squares. Add them to the stack of 2½" squares you have already cut.

2 mark

On the reverse side of each 2½" white square, draw a line from corner to corner once on the diagonal or fold each square in half on the diagonal and press a crease on the fold line to mark your sewing line. Each block uses 7 white squares so you can press/mark as you make each block or press/mark all before beginning to sew in preparation.

3 block construction

Place a marked white square atop a 2½" print square with right sides facing. Sew on the marked line, then trim ¼" away from the sewn seam. **3A**

Add a 1½" x 2½" white strip to the right side of the square. Then sew a 1½" x 3½" white rectangle to the bottom. **3B**

Stitch a 2½" x 3½" print rectangle to the right of the square. Add a matching print 2½" x 5½" rectangle to the bottom. **3C**

Snowball both corners of the block by placing a marked 2½" white square atop the print rectangle with right sides facing. Notice the direction the angles are running. Sew on the marked line, then trim ¼" from the sewn seam. Open and press the seam allowance toward the print fabric. **3D**

Add a 1½" x 5½" white rectangle to the right of the square. Then sew a

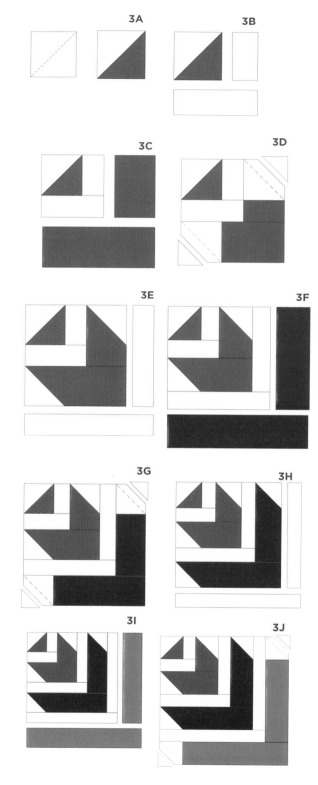

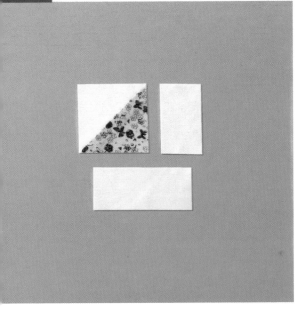

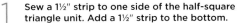

1 Sew a 1½" strip to one side of the half-square triangle unit. Add a 1½" strip to the bottom.

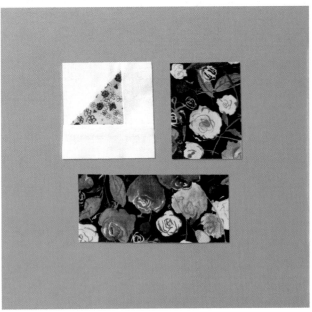

2 Add a 2½" print rectangle to the side and the bottom.

3 Place a 2½" background square on both corners after marking a line from corner to corner once on the diagonal on the reverse side of the square. Sew on the drawn line, then trim ¼" from the sewn seam.

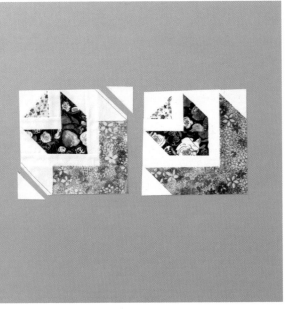

4 After adding 1½" rectangles to the side and the bottom, add 2½" print rectangles. Snowball the upper right and lower left corners by stitching a 2½" marked square to the rectangles. Sew on the drawn lines, trim ¼" from the sewn seam. Open and press.

70

5 Add 1½" rectangles to the side and the bottom of the block. Add 2½" print rectangles, then snowball the upper right and lower left corners as before.

6 Open the snowballed corners and press to complete the block.

1½" x 6½" white rectangle to the bottom of the square. **3E**

Sew a 2½" x 6½" print rectangle to the right of the square and a matching 2½" x 8½" print rectangle to the bottom. **3F**

Snowball both corners of the block by placing a 2½" marked white square atop the two print corners of the block with right sides facing. Sew on the marked line, then trim ¼" away from the sewn seam. Open and press the seam allowance toward the print fabric. **3G**

Sew a 1½" x 8½" white rectangle to the right side of the square. Add a 1½" x 9½" white rectangle to the bottom of the square. **3H**

Stitch a 2½" x 9½" print rectangle to the right side of the square. Add a matching 2½" x 11½" print rectangle to the bottom. **3I**

To complete the block, snowball both corners by placing a 2½" marked white square atop the two print corners of the block with right sides facing. Sew on the marked line, then trim ¼" away from the sewn seam. Open and press the seam allowance toward the print fabric. **3J**
Make 36
Block Size: 11" finished

4 arrange and sew

Lay out the blocks in **6 rows of 6**, paying particular attention to the direction the blocks are placed. See the diagram above. Sew the blocks into rows and press the seam allowances of the odd rows toward the right and the even rows toward the left. Then sew the rows together.

5 inner border

Pick up the (7) 1½" strips you set aside. Sew the strips together end-to-end to make one long strip. Trim the borders from this strip.

Refer to Borders (pg. 102) in the Construction Basics to measure and cut the inner borders. The strips are approximately 66½" for the sides and approximately 68½" for the top and bottom.

6 outer border

Cut (8) 6½" strips across the width of the fabric. Sew the strips together end-

to-end to make one long strip. Trim the borders from this strip.

Refer to Borders (pg. 102) in the Construction Basics to measure and cut the outer borders. The strips are approximately 68½" for the sides and approximately 80½" for the top and bottom.

7 quilt and bind

Layer the quilt with batting and backing and quilt. After the quilting is complete, square up the quilt and trim away all excess batting and backing. Add binding to complete the quilt. See Construction Basics (pg. 102) for binding instructions.

For the tutorial and everything you need to make this quilt visit:
www.msqc.co/blockfall18

on the
fence

Living in Missouri, I find myself absolutely surrounded by German culture. From the town of Hermann, founded in the earliest days of Missouri by German immigrants, to the Amish in nearby Jamesport speaking Pennsylvania Dutch (a dialect of German), you'll find tidbits of German culture and traditions everywhere you look. So, it's no wonder that fall time gets everyone in the mood for Oktoberfest!

David, one of Missouri Star's ad writers, had the wonderful opportunity to live in Germany a few years back. While I've never had the chance to visit, I've always wanted to go to Germany, so he told me all about this wonderful holiday so I could live vicariously through him!

"While the festivals, like the one in Hermann, bring to mind images of barmaids and lederhosen for most folk, Oktoberfest has so much more to offer. It all started out in Germany over 200 years ago. The very first Oktoberfest was actually a wedding! A royal wedding, in fact. Newlywed King Ludwig invited the entire city of Munich to his wedding reception in mid-October to celebrate his marriage to Therese von Sachsen-Hildburghausen (Isn't that a mouthful of a name?) The reception was such a huge success that the people of Munich said, "Wasn't that fun? Why don't we do this every year?"

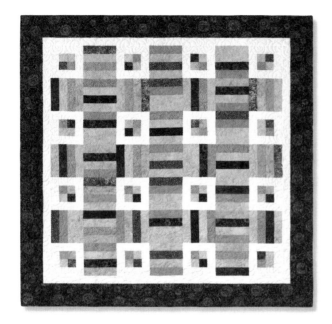

Nowadays, almost seven million people travel to Munich to celebrate Ludwig and Therese's anniversary in the largest Oktoberfest celebration in the world. The festival grounds in Munich fill up with carnival rides for kids and grown-ups alike, live music stages playing everything from traditional German oom-pah-pah to the newest bands, and huge food tents fit to burst with scrumptious German cuisine. Oh, the food! I could go on and on about the delicious pretzels, cheeses, breads, and bratwurst that can be found everywhere you look. The air is so full of mouth-watering scents, every breath you take has its own calorie count!

My favorite food, though, has to be schnitzel. It's a meat dish made of pork, or sometimes veal, that is pounded flat and fried. It's so flavorful and tender, and you'll never have it the same way twice! Every town makes it a little differently. Munich likes to make it pounded nearly paper thin and spiced with paprika and lemon juice, while I had a huge, cheese stuffed schnitzel in Leipzig that was smothered in mushroom gravy and fried potatoes. Oh, what I wouldn't do to have that meal again!"

David's history lesson taught me so much about Oktoberfest, and his descriptions of the food make my mouth water just thinking about it. It makes me want to go pack my bags and go now! Even with this growth from a one day festivity to a worldwide, half-month-long extravaganza, Oktoberfest's message remains the same: a celebration of that same sense of love and community that was there on Ludwig and Therese's wedding day. What's more, Oktoberfest has grown. With celebrations everywhere from Munich to our own Missouri towns, you're never far away from a festival of your own!

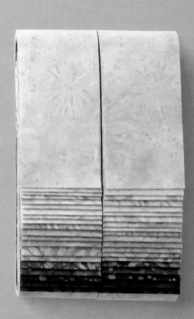

materials

QUILT SIZE
71" x 71"

BLOCK SIZE
8" finished

QUILT TOP
1 roll of 2½" strips
1¼ yards white solid fabric - includes
   inner border

BORDER
1¼ yards

BINDING
¾ yard

BACKING
4½ yards - vertical seam(s)

SAMPLE QUILT
A Shore Thing by Wilmington Prints

1 cut

From the white solid fabric, cut:

• (11) 2½" strips across the width of
  the fabric – subcut each strip into (3)
  2½" x 8½" rectangles and (3) 2½" x
  4½" rectangles. A **total of 32** of each
  size of rectangle is needed.

2 make strip sets

Select (4) 2½" strips from the roll. Sew
them together along the length. Press all
seam allowances in the same direction.
Make 9 strips sets. Cut (4) 8½" squares
from each strip set. Each strip set will
yield 4 blocks and a **total of 33** are

needed. **2A**

2A

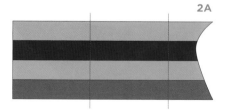

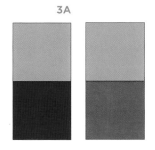

3A

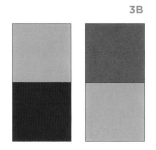

3B

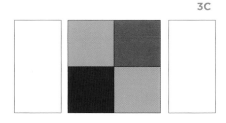

3C

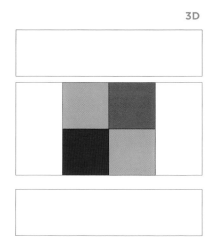

3D

Eight of the strips sets will have at least a 6″ piece left over. (The amount left over depends on the width of the fabric.) From those pieces, cut:

- (2) 2½″ x 8½″ strips. A **total of 16** are needed

From the last strip, there will be about 31″ left. Cut the piece into 2½″ increments and set aside to use when making the bonus table runner. The strip will yield 12 pieces.

3 bordered 4-patch blocks

Pick up the stack of 2½″ x 8½″ strip sets. Remove the stitches between the second and third pieces. You will have (2) 2-patches. **3A**

Sew the 2-patches into a 4-patch as shown. **3B**

Sew a 2½″ x 4½″ rectangle to either side of a 4-patch. **3C**

Add a 2½″ x 8½″ rectangle to the top and the bottom to complete the block. **Make 16. 3D**
Block Size: 8″ finished

4 arrange and sew

Lay out the blocks in rows. Each row is made up of **7 blocks** and there are **7 rows.** Rows 1, 3, 5, and 7 begin with a bordered 4-patch and alternate with a strip set block. All other rows are made

using strip set blocks. Refer to the diagram on page 79 and be aware of the direction in which the strip set blocks are turned.

After the blocks have been sewn into rows, press the seam allowances of the odd rows toward the right and the even rows toward the left. This will help the seams "nest." Sew the rows together to complete the center of the quilt.

5 inner border

Cut (6) 2½″ strips across the width of the fabric. Sew the strips together end-to-end to make one long strip. Trim the borders from this strip.

Refer to Borders (pg. 102) in the Construction Basics to measure and cut the inner borders. The strips are approximately 56½″ for the sides and approximately 60½″ for the top and bottom.

6 outer border

Cut (7) 6″ strips across the width of the fabric. Sew the strips together end-to-end to make one long strip. Trim the borders from this strip.

Refer to Borders (pg. 102) in the Construction Basics to measure and cut the outer borders. The strips are approximately 60½″ for the sides and approximately 71½″ for the top and bottom.

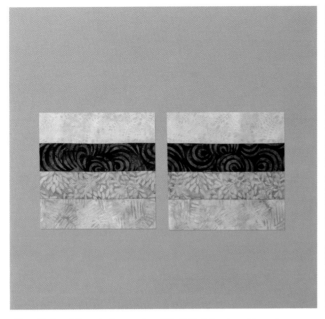

1 Make strip sets by sewing (4) 2½″ strips together along the length. Press all seam allowances in the same direction, then cut 8½″ squares from each strip set.

2 Cut 2½″ increments from the remaining 6″ piece of the strip sets. Remove the stitches between the second and third pieces to make (2) 2-patches.

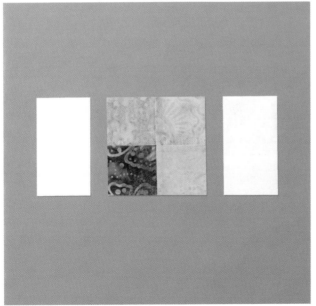

3 Sew the 2-patches together to make a 4-patch. Add a 2½″ x 4½″ rectangle to either side of the 4-patch.

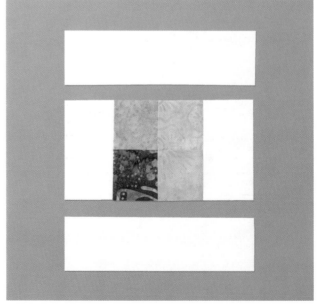

4 Add a 2½″ x 8½″ rectangle to the top and bottom to complete the block.

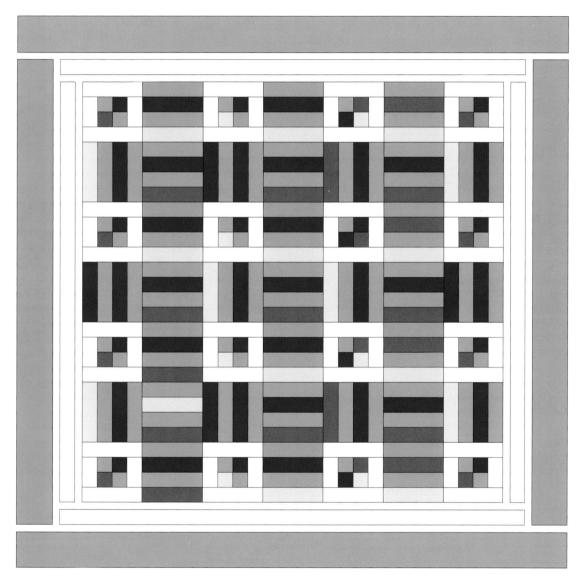

7 quilt and bind

Layer the quilt with batting and backing and quilt. After the quilting is complete, square up the quilt and trim away all excess batting and backing. Add binding to complete the quilt. See Construction Basics (pg. 102) for binding instructions.

Bonus Project: Table Runner

materials

TABLE RUNNER SIZE
18" x 46"

TABLE RUNNER TOP
(3) 2½" print strips – Use leftover strips
(12) 2½" x 8½" strip set pieces – Use the pieces previously cut from the strip sets
¾ yard white solid fabric – includes border

BINDING
½ yard

BACKING
1½ yards - vertical seam(s)

SAMPLE QUILT
A Shore Thing by Wilmington Prints

1 cut

From the white fabric, cut:

* (6) 2½" strips across the width of the fabric – subcut each strip into (2) 2½" x 14½" rectangles for a total of 12. Set the rest of the fabric aside for the top and bottom border.

2 sew

Make a strip set by sewing the 3 print 2½" strips together along the length. Press the seam allowances all in the same direction. Cut the strip set into 2½" increments. A **total of 11** are needed. **2A**

3 block construction

Pick up the strip set pieces made using 4 strips that you set aside earlier. Sew a strip set that's made up of 3 squares to 1 made up of 4 squares. There will be 7 squares in the block. **Make 11 blocks. 3A**

Block Size: 2" x 14" finished

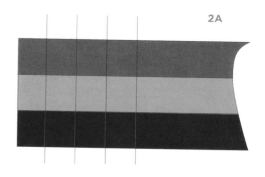

2A

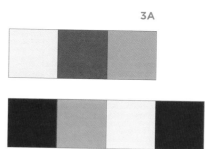

3A

Sew a white 2½" x 14½" rectangle to each side of a strip set block. Add a strip set, then another white rectangle. Continue on in this manner until you have sewn 12 white rectangles and 11 strip sets together. Refer to the diagram to the left.

From the remaining white fabric, cut:

- (3) 2½" strips across the width of the fabric. Sew the strips together end-to-end. Measure the table runner through the center. It should measure approximately 46½". Cut 2 pieces from the strip to equal your measurement. Sew a strip to each long side of the table runner.

4 quilt and bind

Layer the table runner with batting and backing and quilt. After the quilting is complete, square up the runner and trim away all excess batting and backing. Add binding to complete. See Construction Basics (pg. 102) for binding instructions.

jumping
jacks

Amber grew up in a family of considerable size: Four brothers, three sisters, Mom, Dad, and grandparents just across the street. With so many people in the house, birthdays came 'round almost as often as the Sunday paper.

That seemingly endless stream of cupcakes and candles might seem like a dream come true for any kid, but there was just one problem: Amber didn't at all care for cake at all.

But, as luck would have it, Amber had been born during the loveliest of seasons: harvest time. Every year as late summer slowly melted into fall, Amber's birthday was celebrated with a fresh-baked peach pie.

The peaches were plucked from a tree in her very own backyard. They were the biggest, prettiest peaches you've ever seen, and they always ripened just in time for Amber's birthday.

For the tutorial and everything you need to make this quilt visit:
www.msqc.co/blockfall18

But one year, after a particularly heavy snowfall, the two main branches of the peach tree crashed to the ground, splitting the tree in two. After that, Amber still got her birthday pie, but it was made with plain ole store-bought peaches, and it just wasn't the same.

Years passed, and Amber was preparing to celebrate her 25th birthday at home with her family and her very ordinary peaches. But fate had something more in store. A new young man had walked into her life, and he brought with him a slice of peach pie.

On their first date, Kyle packed a lunch of fried chicken, homemade rolls, potato salad, and fresh peach pie— all from his own family's restaurant. They drove to a beautiful spot overlooking the fall colors that blanketed the valley. Everything tasted wonderful, but there was something about that pie! Whether it was the buttery crust, the perfectly sweet peaches, or the piercing blue of Kyle's eyes, we'll never know. But one year later, that pie was served at their wedding, and it's been sweetening Amber's birthday every year since.

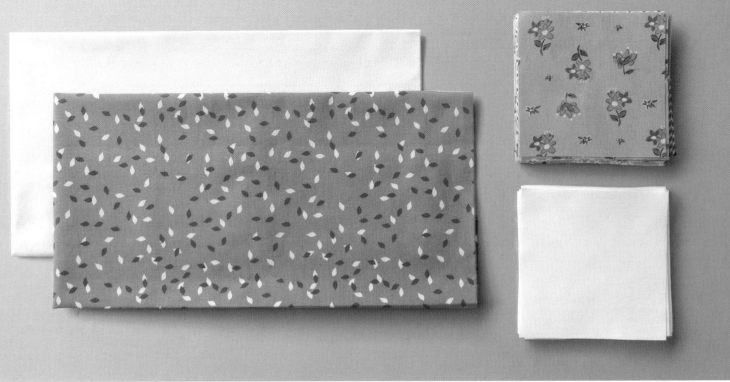

materials

QUILT SIZE
55" x 69" finished

BLOCK SIZE
7" x 8" finished

QUILT TOP
2 matching packages 5" print squares
2 packages 5" background squares

INNER BORDER
½ yard

OUTER BORDER
1 yard

BINDING
¾ yard

BACKING
3½ yards - horizontal seam(s)

SAMPLE QUILT
Summer Blush by Sedef Imer for Riley Blake Designs

1 make half-square triangles

Draw a line from corner to corner once on the diagonal on the reverse side of the 5" background squares. Select 2 matching 5" print squares. Layer each with a marked background square, with right sides facing. Sew on both sides of the drawn line using a ¼" seam allowance. Cut on the drawn line and open to reveal 2 half-square triangles. Press the seam allowance to the darker side. Square each half-square triangle unit to 4½" and keep all matching half-square triangles stacked together. **1A**

Make 168 half-square triangles.

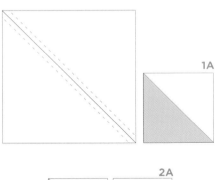

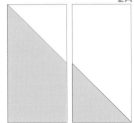

2B

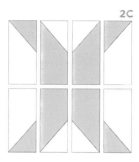

2C

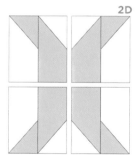

2D

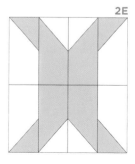

2E

2 block construction

Select 4 matching half-square triangles. Cut 2 with the diagonal going from lower right to upper left to make 2¼" x 4½" rectangles. 2A

Cut the remaining 2 with the diagonal going from lower left to upper right to make 2¼" x 4½" rectangles. 2B

Lay out the 8 pieces as shown. Notice that the portion of the half-square triangle that has a small triangle showing has been flipped 180° and has traded places with the other side. 2C

Sew each half-square triangle unit back together after the pieces have been rearranged. 2D

Sew the 4 units together as shown to complete the block. **Make 42 blocks.** 2E

Block size: 7" x 8" finished.

3 arrange and sew

Arrange the blocks in rows. Each row is made up of **6 blocks** and a **total of 7 rows** are needed. Press the seam allowances of the odd rows toward the left and the even rows toward the right. This will make the seams "nest." Sew the rows together to complete the center portion of the quilt.

4 inner border

Cut (6) 2½" strips across the width of the fabric. Sew the strips together end-to-end to make one long strip. Trim the borders from this strip.

Refer to Borders (pg. 102) in the Construction Basics to measure and cut the inner borders. The strips are approximately 56½" for the sides and approximately 46½" for the top and bottom.

5 outer border

Cut (6) 5" strips across the width of the fabric. Sew the strips together end-to-end to make one long strip. Trim the borders from this strip.

Refer to Borders (pg. 102) in the Construction Basics to measure and cut the outer borders. The strips are approximately 60½" for the sides and approximately 55½" for the top and bottom.

6 quilt and bind

Layer the quilt with batting and backing and quilt. After the quilting is complete, square up the quilt and trim away all excess batting and backing. Add binding to complete the quilt. See Construction Basics (pg. 102) for binding instructions.

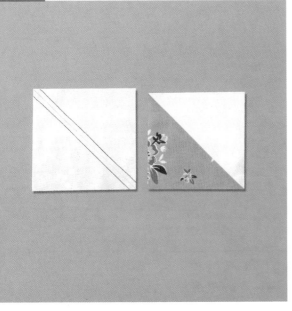

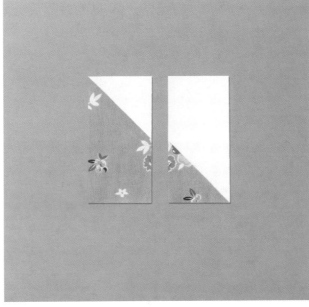

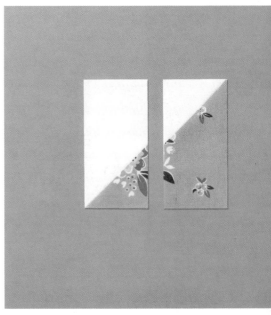

1 Draw a line from corner to corner once on the diagonal on the reverse side of a 5″ background square. Layer the marked square with a print square and sew on both sides of the line using a ¼″ seam allowance. Cut on the drawn line, open to reveal 2 half-square triangles.

2 Cut 2 half-square triangle units in half vertically with the diagonal going from lower right to upper left to make 2¼″ x 4½″ rectangles.

3 Cut 2 half-square triangles in half vertically with the diagonal going from lower left to upper right to make 2¼″ x 4½″ rectangles.

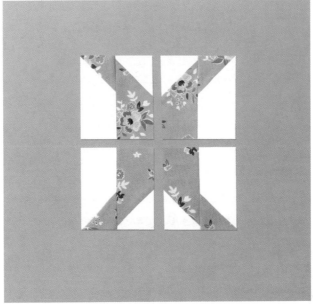

4 Lay out the 8 rectangles as shown.

5 Sew the rectangles together into 4 quadrants.

6 Sew the quadrants together to complete the block.

playful
new prints
from
missouri
star

Have you seen Missouri Star's fun new line of fabrics? With playful prints featuring our famous quacking duck and inspiring phrases in bright, beautiful colors, these darling fabrics are a blast to work with! We've put together a few projects full of Missouri Star spirit that we think you're going to love. Showcase them at your next retreat or guild meeting and you'll be the talk of the town.

Tote along your favorite tools or supplies in a cute, reversible bag. This friendly project makes a great gift, too. Stitch it up for your friends and make them smile. No matter how you use our new Missouri Star fabrics, we hope you have a lot of fun!

reversible bag

BAG SIZE: 11½" x 11½"

SUPPLY LIST
½ yard of fabric 1
¾ yard of fabric 2 - includes fabric for strap
1½" x 40" strip of lightweight quilt batting

1 cut
From each piece of fabric, cut:
- (3) 12" squares

From fabric #2, cut:
- (1) 5" x 40" strip across the width of the fabric – this will be used for the strap.

2 fold and sew
Fold (1) 12" square of each fabric in half with wrong sides facing and press to make a pocket. Align the sides and the bottom of the pocket made with fabric #1 with a 12" square using fabric #2. Pin in place. Divide the pocket into 2 or 3 sections, and mark. We sectioned ours off into 3 sections that measured 3" in from one side and 4" in from the other.

Stitch the pocket sections using a straight stitch. Be sure to back stitch at the top of the pocket where it will get the most wear. Measure up 2" from the bottom of the pocket and stitch a straight line all the way across.

This completes the front of the bag.

Layer the remaining 12" square cut from fabric #2 with the front of the bag with right sides facing. Sew down one side, across the bottom, and up the other side using a ¼" seam allowance.

Repeat using the remaining 12" squares. You should have 2 squares cut from fabric #1 and 1 square cut from fabric #2. Make the pocket using fabric #2 and the front and back of the bag using fabric #1. Stitch together as before. You should have 2 bags now. Leave them turned wrong side out.

3 make boxed corners
Place your hand inside the body of one of the bags. Push the corner out and align the side seam with the bottom seam. A peak will form.

Measure 1¾" from the point of the peak and draw a line straight across. Sew on the drawn line, then trim the excess fabric away ¼" from the sewn seam. Repeat for the other corner of the bag. **3A**

Box the corners of the second bag using the same measurements. We want them to match up!

While the bags are wrong side out, turn the top raw edge over about ½" and press.

4 make the strap
Pick up the 5" x 40" strip cut earlier and trim the selvages off. Fold the strip in half lengthwise with wrong sides together. Press. Open the strap and press both raw edges in (about ½") toward the center crease.

Open one of the folded edges and place the 1½" x 40" strip of batting between the center of the strip and the fold. Fold the strip in half along the center pressed crease and stitch the strap closed by sewing

¼" from the edge. Add two more lines of stitching by sewing ¼" in from the opposite edge and right down the center. Trim the ends of the strap to your desired length.

5 putting it all together
Turn one of the bags right side out. Slide the remaining bag inside, aligning the side seams. The wrong sides should be touching.

Pin the tops of the bags together so the edges meet. Slide the ends of the strap between the 2 fabric layers, centering each end of the strap directly over opposite side seams. After making sure the strap is straight, pin in place.

Complete the bag by top stitching around the top. **5A**

3A

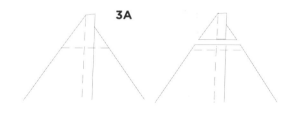

5A

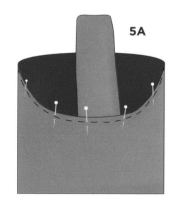

54-40 or fight freestyle

QUILT SIZE
75" x 75"

BLOCK SIZE
12" finished

QUILT TOP
1 package of 10" print squares
3¼ yards background fabric
   - includes inner border

OUTER BORDER
1½ yards

BINDING
¾ yard

BACKING
4¾ yards - vertical seam(s)

SAMPLE QUILT
Twilight by One Canoe Two for
Moda Fabrics

QUILTING PATTERN
Wind Swirls

ONLINE TUTORIALS
msqc.co/blockfall18

PATTERN
pg. 6

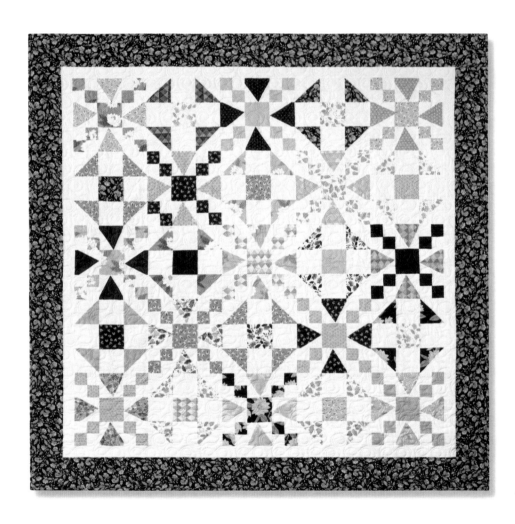

jenny's doll quilt

QUILT SIZE
26" x 26"

BLOCK SIZE
10" finished

QUILT TOP
1 package of 5" print squares
½ yard background fabric
   - includes cornerstones
½ yard white solid

BINDING
½ yard

BACKING
1 yard

SAMPLE QUILT
Guest Room by Kristyne Czepuryk of
Pretty by Hand for Moda Fabrics

QUILTING PATTERN
Stars and Loops

ONLINE TUTORIALS
msqc.co/blockfall18

PATTERN
pg. 56

jitterbug

QUILT SIZE
71" X 71"

BLOCK SIZE
24" finished

QUILT TOP
1 package 5" squares
1½ yards medium blue solid
2 yards white
½ yard medium blue print

BORDER
1¼ yards

BINDING
¾ yard

BACKING
4½ yards - vertical seam(s)

SAMPLE QUILT
Garden Side Path by Rebecca Baer
for Robert Kaufman Fabrics

QUILTING PATTERN
Variety

ONLINE TUTORIALS
msqc.co/blockfall18

PATTERN
pg. 48

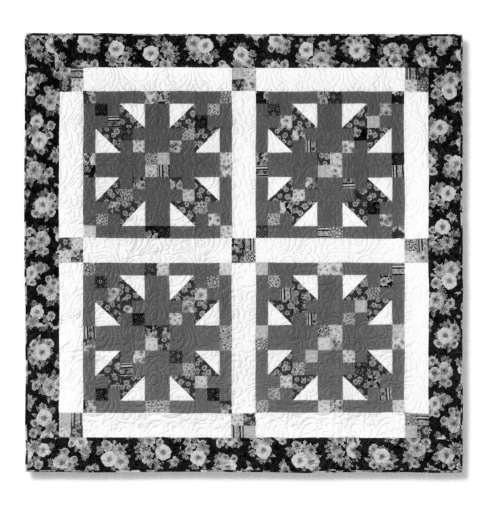

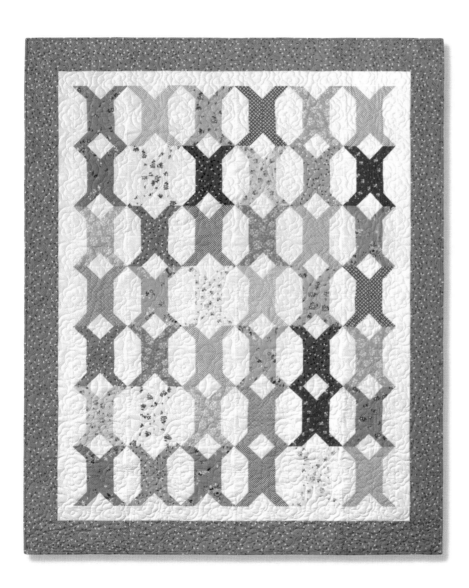

jumping jacks

QUILT SIZE
55″ x 69″ finished

BLOCK SIZE
7″ x 8″ finished

QUILT TOP
2 matching packages 5″ print squares
2 packages 5″ background squares

INNER BORDER
½ yard

OUTER BORDER
1 yard

BINDING
¾ yard

BACKING
3½ yards - horizontal seam(s)

SAMPLE QUILT
Summer Blush by Sedef Imer for Riley Blake Designs

QUILTING PATTERN
Simply Roses

ONLINE TUTORIALS
msqc.co/blockfall18

PATTERN
pg. 82

kite
season

QUILT SIZE
88" x 94"

BLOCK SIZE
8" x 13" finished

QUILT TOP
1 package of 10" print squares
3¾ yards of background fabric
   - includes inner border

BORDER
1¾ yards

BINDING
¾ yard

BACKING
8 yards - horizontal seam(s)
   - or 3 yards 108" wide

SAMPLE QUILT
Road Trippin by Terri Degenkolb for
Windham Fabrics

QUILTING PATTERN
Cotton Candy

ONLINE TUTORIALS
msqc.co/blockfall18

PATTERN
pg. 32

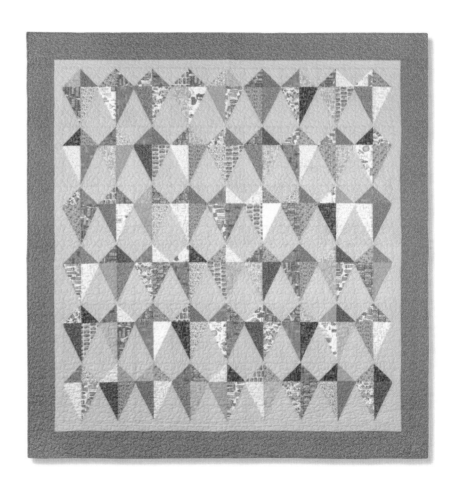

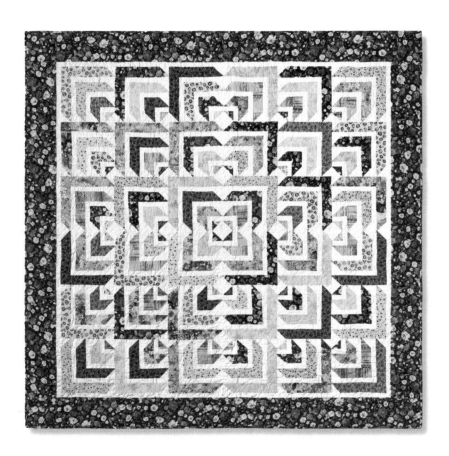

north star

QUILT SIZE
80" x 80"

BLOCK SIZE
11" finished

QUILT TOP
1 roll 1½" white strips - includes inner
  border
1 roll 2½" print strips
3 packages of 2½" squares - 84 count

BORDER
1¾ yards

BINDING
¾ yard

BACKING
7½ yards - vertical seam(s)
  or 2½ yards 108" wide

SAMPLE QUILT
Petal Park by RJR Fabrics

QUILTING PATTERN
Simply Roses

ONLINE TUTORIALS
msqc.co/blockfall18

PATTERN
pg. 64

on the fence

QUILT SIZE
71" x 71"

BLOCK SIZE
8" finished

QUILT TOP
1 roll of 2½" strips
1¼ yards white solid fabric - includes
   inner border

BORDER
1¼ yards

BINDING
¾ yard

BACKING
4½ yards - vertical seam(s)

SAMPLE QUILT
A Shore Thing by Wilmington Prints

QUILTING PATTERN
Free Swirls

ONLINE TUTORIALS
msqc.co/blockfall18

PATTERN
pg. 72

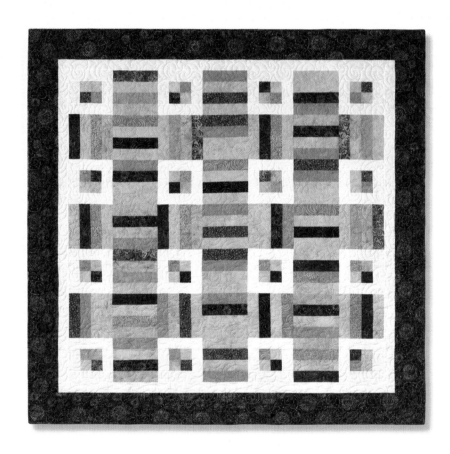

royal wedding

QUILT SIZE
69" x 69"

BLOCK SIZE
18" finished

QUILT TOP
1 package of 10" print squares
½ yard white

BORDER
2 yards - includes sashing strips
  and block pieces

BINDING
¾ yard

BACKING
4¼ yards - vertical seam(s)

SAMPLE QUILT
Wild Bouquet by Citrus and Mint
Designs for RIley Blake Designs

QUILTING PATTERN
Paisley Feather

ONLINE TUTORIALS
msqc.co/blockfall18

PATTERN
pg. 24

summer camp

QUILT SIZE
62" X 78"

BLOCK SIZE
8" finished

QUILT TOP
1 roll of 2½" print strips
1¼ yards background fabric
  – includes inner border
¾ yard complimentary solid fabric

OUTER BORDER
1¼ yards

BINDING
¾ yard

BACKING
4¾ yards - vertical seam(s)

SAMPLE QUILT
Road Trip by Alison Glass for
Andover Fabrics

QUILTING PATTERN
Variety

ONLINE TUTORIALS
msqc.co/blockfall18

PATTERN
pg. 16

treasure box

QUILT SIZE
39" x 44"

BLOCK SIZE
5" finished

QUILT TOP
1 package 5" print or solid squares
1 package 5" background squares

INNER BORDER
¼ yard

OUTER BORDER
½ yard

BINDING
½ yard

BACKING
3 yards - vertical seam(s)

SAMPLE QUILT
Top Drawer by Kathy Hall for
Andover Fabrics

QUILTING PATTERN
Variety

ONLINE TUTORIALS
msqc.co/blockfall18

PATTERN
pg. 40

construction basics

general quilting

- All seams are ¼" inch unless directions specify differently.
- Cutting instructions are given at the point when cutting is required.
- Precuts are not prewashed; therefore do not prewash other fabrics in the project.
- All strips are cut width of fabric.
- Remove all selvages.

press seams

- Use a steam iron on the cotton setting.
- Press the seam just as it was sewn right sides together. This "sets" the seam.
- With dark fabric on top, lift the dark fabric and press back.
- The seam allowance is pressed toward the dark side. Some patterns may direct otherwise for certain situations.
- Follow pressing arrows in the diagrams when indicated.
- Press toward borders. Pieced borders may demand otherwise.
- Press diagonal seams open on binding to reduce bulk.

borders

- Always measure the quilt top 3 times before cutting borders.
- Start measuring about 4" in from each side and through the center vertically.
- Take the average of those 3 measurements.
- Cut 2 border strips to that size. Piece strips together if needed.
- Attach one to either side of the quilt.

- Position the border fabric on top as you sew. The feed dogs can act like rufflers. Having the border on top will prevent waviness and keep the quilt straight.
- Repeat this process for the top and bottom borders, measuring the width 3 times.
- Include the newly attached side borders in your measurements.
- Press toward the borders.

binding

find a video tutorial at: www.msqc.co/006

- Use 2½" strips for binding.
- Sew strips end-to-end into one long strip with diagonal seams, aka the plus sign method (next). Press seams open.
- Fold in half lengthwise wrong sides together and press.
- The entire length should equal the outside dimension of the quilt plus 15" - 20."

plus sign method

- Lay one strip across the other as if to make a plus sign right sides together.
- Sew from top inside to bottom outside corners crossing the intersections of fabric as you sew.
  Trim excess to ¼" seam allowance.
- Press seam open.

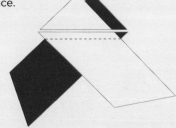

find a video tutorial at: www.msqc.co/001

attach binding

- Match raw edges of folded binding to the quilt top edge.
- Leave a 10″ tail at the beginning.
- Use a ¼″ seam allowance.
- Start in the middle of a long straight side.

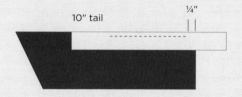

10″ tail   ¼″

miter corners

- Stop sewing ¼″ before the corner.
- Move the quilt out from under the presser foot.
- Clip the threads.
- Flip the binding up at a 90° angle to the edge just sewn.
- Fold the binding down along the next side to be sewn, aligning raw edges.
- The fold will lie along the edge just completed.
- Begin sewing on the fold.

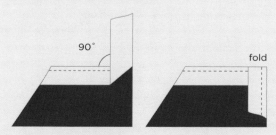

90°   fold

close binding

MSQC recommends The Binding Tool from TQM Products to finish binding perfectly every time.

- Stop sewing when you have 12″ left to reach the start.
- Where the binding tails come together, trim excess leaving only 2½″ of overlap.
- It helps to pin or clip the quilt together at the two points where the binding starts and stops. This takes the pressure off of the binding tails while you work.
- Use the plus sign method to sew the two binding ends together, except this time when making the plus sign, match the edges. Using a pencil, mark your sewing line because you won't be able to see where the corners intersect. Sew across.

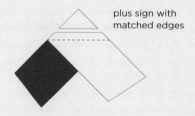

plus sign with matched edges

- Trim off excess; press seam open.
- Fold in half wrong sides together, and align all raw edges to the quilt top.
- Sew this last binding section to the quilt. Press.
- Turn the folded edge of the binding around to the back of the quilt and tack into place with an invisible stitch or machine stitch if you wish.